U...E INTRODUCTION TO MUSIC

Eileen O'Brien

Designed by Melissa Alaverdy
and Laura Fearn

Edited by Jane Chisholm

Additional material: Caroline Hooper

Managing designer: Stephen Wright

Illustrations: Aziz Khan and Luigi Galante

Cover design: Zoë Wray and Tom Lalonde

Digital images: John Russell

Picture research: Ruth King

CONTENTS

LISTENING TO MUSIC

You don't need to know much about a piece of music to enjoy it. But you may find you appreciate it more if you know a little about why it was written and how it achieves its effect. This book explains what is interesting about a whole range of musical styles - pop, blues, classical - so that you know what to listen for, and how different sorts of music developed. Once you know more about it, you may even find you like types of music that you never liked before.

As each style of music is introduced, there are suggestions for music to listen to. You can now listen to all kinds of music on the Internet, without having to go out and buy a recording. Find out more about this on pages 86-89.

WHAT MAKES MUSIC?

A piece of music is made up of lots of different elements. How it sounds depends on which of these are used and how they are combined. For instance, you could probably identify a 1950s rock and roll song just from the rhythm, the instruments used, and the style of singing.

BEAT OR PULSE

If you clap along to a piece of music, you usually find yourself clapping on the beat, or pulse.

RHYTHM

Rhythm is a pattern of long and short sounds and silences which fit around the beat.

MELODY

The melody or tune is the part which you might whistle or sing. It is a pattern of sounds, called notes, of different pitches. The pitch of a note is how high or low it sounds.

STRUCTURE

The structure is what makes the music sound organized. Most structures are based on repetition and variation of a theme or tune.

HARMONY

A chord is two or more notes sung or played together. The way that chords are made up and fit together in music is called harmony. Harmony is often used to make music sound more interesting.

TONE QUALITY

Each instrument has its own special sound, or tone. The instruments chosen for a piece of music give it a certain sound. This is called *timbre*, or tone quality.

EXPRESSION

Music played without energy and feeling sounds dead. A musician uses contrasts in volume, emphasis and so on to express the mood of the music and add vitality.

INTERNET LINKS

This book contains descriptions of more than 100 websites where you can find out more about music. To visit the sites, go to the **Usborne Quicklinks Website** at www.usborne-quicklinks.com and type the keywords "intro to music". There you will find links to click on to take you to all the sites. Here are some of the things you can do on the recommended sites:

• Listen to samples of rock, jazz, reggae and many other music genres

• Play music games and make music online with an interactive sound mixer

• Hear sound clips of different musical instruments

• Watch video clips and listen to music from famous ballets and operas

INTERNET SAFETY

When using the Internet, please make sure you follow these guidelines:

• Ask your parent's or guardian's permission before you connect to the Internet.

• If you write a message in a website guest book or on a website message board, do not include any personal information such as your full name, address or telephone number, and ask an adult before you give your email address.

• If a website asks you to log in or register by typing your name or e-mail address, ask permission of an adult first.

• If you do receive an email from someone you don't know, tell an adult and do not reply to the email.

• Never arrange to meet anyone you have talked to on the Internet.

SITE AVAILABILITY

The links in **Usborne Quicklinks** are regularly reviewed and updated, but occasionally you may get a message that a site is unavailable. This might be temporary, so try again later, or even the next day. Websites do occasionally close down and when this happens, we will replace them with new links in **Usborne Quicklinks**. Sometimes we add extra links too, if we think they are useful. So when you visit **Usborne Quicklinks**, the links may be slightly different from those described in your book.

DOWNLOADABLE PICTURES

Pictures in this book marked with a ★ symbol can be downloaded from **Usborne Quicklinks** for your own personal use, for example, to illustrate a homework report or project. The pictures are the copyright of Usborne Publishing and may not be used for any commercial or profit-related purpose. To download a picture, go to **Usborne Quicklinks** and follow the instructions there.

NOTE FOR PARENTS AND GUARDIANS

The websites described in this book are regularly reviewed and the links in **Usborne Quicklinks** are updated. However, the content of a website may change at any time and Usborne Publishing is not responsible for the content on any website other than its own. We recommend that children are supervised while on the Internet, that they do not use Internet Chat Rooms, and that you use Internet filtering software to block unsuitable material. Please ensure that your children read and follow the safety guidelines printed on the left. For more information, see the "Net Help" area on the **Usborne Quicklinks Website**.

USING THE INTERNET

For downloadable pictures and links to all the websites described in this book, follow these steps:

1. Go to **www.usborne-quicklinks.com**

2. Type the keywords for this book: **intro to music**

3. Type the page number of the links you want to visit.

4. Click on the links to go to the recommended sites

WHAT YOU NEED

To visit the websites you need a computer with an Internet connection and a web browser (the software that lets you look at information on the Internet). Some sites need extra programs (plug-ins) to play sound or show videos or animations.

EXTRAS

Some websites need additional free programs, called plug-ins, to play sounds, or to show videos, animations or 3-D images. For instance, lots of the sites in this book include music to listen to, and you may need to download a plug-in to listen to it. (To find out more about how to listen to music on the Internet, see pages 86-89.) If you go to a site and you do not have the necessary plug-in, a message saying so will come up on the screen. There is usually a button on the site that you can click on to download the plug-in. Alternatively, go to the **Usborne Quicklinks Website** at **www.usborne-quicklinks.com** and click on "Net Help". There you can find links to download plug-ins.

Here is a list of plug-ins that you might need:
RealonePlayer® – lets you play video and hear sound files
QuickTime – enables you to view video clips
Flash™ – lets you play animations
Shockwave® – lets you play animations and interactive programs

HELP

For general help and advice on using the Internet, go to **Usborne Quicklinks** at **www.usborne-quicklinks.com** and click on "Net Help".

To find out more about how to use your Web browser, click on "Help" at the top of the browser, and then choose "Contents and Index". You'll find a huge searchable dictionary containing tips on how to find your way around the Internet easily.

COMPUTER VIRUSES

A computer virus is a program that can seriously damage your computer. A virus can get into your computer when you download programs from the Internet, or in an attachment (an extra file) that arrives with an email. We strongly recommend that you buy special software called anti-virus software to protect your computer and that you update the software regularly.

Internet link

For a link to a website where you can find out more about computer viruses, go to **www.usborne-quicklinks.com**

TYPES OF MUSIC

You can listen to all kinds of music on the Net: classical, rock, jazz, to name just a few. Some of these mean different things to different people, or change their meaning as time goes by. But most people tend to classify music loosely as either classical or popular. Throughout this book, you'll find suggestions for websites where you can listen to particular styles of music.

These Chinese drummers are performing as part of the Chinese New Year celebrations. You can find out about music in the Far East on pages 38-39.

POPULAR MUSIC

Popular music is a general term for what most people listen to for entertainment. It tends to rely on a catchy melody and a strong rhythm. It usually means any type of music - jazz, pop, rock - which is not classified as 'serious' or 'classical'.

TRADITIONAL MUSIC

Traditional music (also known as folk, or world, music) is the national popular music of any country. The origins of many traditional styles go back hundreds of years.

Traditional music is not usually written down, but passed on, just by being played, from one generation to the next. Lots of this type of music is improvised: the players make up the music, or part of it, as they go along. You can find out about different styles of traditional music on pages 38-43.

Since the 1980s, Madonna has been one of the world's most successful pop singers.

A CD by the American rap artist Lauryn Hill, called *The Miseducation of Lauryn Hill*. You can read about rap on page 13.

ROCK AND POP MUSIC

People use the terms 'rock' and 'pop' to mean different things. Pop is short for 'popular music', but it usually only means music that has been in the charts, now or in the past. Rock is a particular style of music that first developed in the 1960s. Nowadays it is used as a more general term, to describe several different categories of pop music, such as reggae, punk or heavy metal. You can read about some different types of rock and pop on pages 10-13.

JAZZ

Jazz began in the early 1900s in the southern states of the U.S., but has since evolved into several different styles. Some are easy to listen to. Others are more complex, but many people find these the most exciting. A lot of jazz is improvised, which means that each musician brings his or her own ideas to a piece. You can find out more about jazz on pages 16-19.

CLASSICAL MUSIC

Most people use the term 'classical music' rather loosely, for serious or formal music, performed in front of a seated, silent audience. Its origins go back to religious music and music written to entertain aristocrats and wealthy people in their own homes.

Strictly speaking, though, the term 'Classical' only applies to European music of the second half of the 18th century. In this book, music from this period is called Classical, with a capital C. Styles of classical music from other periods have their own names, such as Baroque, Nationalist or Romantic music. All these styles are described later in the book.

ROCK AND POP

Rock and pop is more than just music to listen or dance to. It sets and reflects young people's lifestyles and trends. This idea didn't really exist until the 1950s, when a new style of music exploded onto the scene in the U.S., setting off a craze among teenagers. The new music was called rock and roll, and it paved the way for all the different rock and pop styles that have emerged since.

Sun Records signed up lots of famous rock and roll names of the 50s, including Elvis Presley.

THE BIRTH OF ROCK AND ROLL

From the 17th century, millions of Africans were taken to the southern states of America and the Caribbean, and sold as slaves. The slaves brought their own style of music with them from Africa. Over time, this music evolved into new styles, such as blues and gospel.

In the early 1900s, millions of African Americans moved to cities in search of work. In the 1950s, the mixture of different styles of music they played, amplified and accompanied by electric instruments, developed into something that would change the face of popular music: rhythm and blues, or R&B.

Internet link

For a link to a website where you can take a virtual tour of Sun Records to find out about its famous performers, go to **www.usborne-quicklinks.com**

In the mid-1950s, white American teenagers began to listen to R&B performers such as Chuck Berry. Soon, lots of white performers began to use elements of R&B in their music. Elvis Presley and groups such as Bill Haley and the Comets became very successful when they combined R&B with country music. This was the beginning of rock and roll.

Elvis Presley (1935-1977) was probably the most successful rock and roll star of the 1950s.

OTHER INFLUENCES

Although the greatest influence on rock and pop has come from African American music, rock borrows elements from other styles too. For example, the scales and harmonies on which most pop is based came into use in 18th century classical music, and some bands use orchestral instruments, such as violins.

Pop also borrows from the traditional music of Europe, the Far East and other places. During the mid-1960s, the Beatles became interested in Indian music and its influence can be heard in lots of their songs. More recently, bands such as the Corrs have used traditional Irish instruments in their music.

Sharon Corr, from the Corrs, playing the fiddle. The band also uses an Irish drum called a bodhrán, as well as a flute.

The Beatles gave some of their songs an exotic quality by using Indian instruments, such as the sitar, shown here.

This picture is taken from the Beatles' 1967 album, *Sgt. Pepper's Lonely Hearts Club Band*. On this album, George Harrison (far right) plays the sitar and another Indian stringed instrument called a tambura.

POPULAR MUSIC STYLES

Popular music changes all the time, as each new generation of musicians reacts to a changing world. The most successful musicians take elements from different types of music and combine them to form something new and original. Over the next few pages, you can read about the roots of some of the main styles of popular music.

This type of guitar, called the Dobro resonator guitar, is popular with many blues artists.

Music to listen to (the suggestions are all albums)

BLUES
Bessie Smith, *The Essential Bessie Smith* (1923)
John Lee Hooker, *I'm John Lee Hooker* (1960)

GOSPEL
Marion Williams, *Born to Sing Gospel* (1995)
The Edwin Hawkins Singers, *The Best of the Edwin Hawkins Singers* (1997)

JAZZ
King Oliver, *1923* (1994)
Duke Ellington, *The Carnegie Hall Concerts: December 1944* (1944)

R&B
Isley Brothers, *Twist and Shout* (1962)

BLUES

Blues was first played by African Americans in the early 1900s in the southern states of the U.S. The word 'blues' also means a sad or melancholy state of mind, and many blues songs tell of the hard lives led by the people.

B.B. King, one of the world's most influential blues musicians

GOSPEL

Gospel songs were first sung around the end of the 19th century by African slaves who converted to Christianity. The joyful, emotional style which developed from these songs thrives in lots of churches in the southern states of the U.S. People often clap their hands or stamp their feet to the music.

JAZZ

Like blues, jazz also appeared at the beginning of the 20th century, and was first played in and around New Orleans.

R&B

R&B (rhythm and blues) is a style of music that was first played by Black people in the late 1940s. It grew out of blues and gospel, and began mainly as dance music. R&B contains elements of jazz, in particular its driving rhythm.

10

ROCK AND ROLL

The main roots of rock and roll lie in country music and R&B. Early performers include Buddy Holly, the Everly Brothers and Elvis Presley. Rock and roll usually has a strong rhythmic drive, to encourage listeners to dance. This was one of the reasons why it made such a strong impact on teenagers during the 1950s and 60s.

Internet links

For links to websites where you can hear clips from famous blues artists and listen to an online traditional music radio station, go to **www.usborne-quicklinks.com**

SOUL

Soul is a mixture of gospel and R&B. During the 1960s and 70s, though, soul was used as a name for almost any African American music. There are different types of soul, including funk and disco. Some styles are named after the record label associated with the sound, such as Motown, Philadelphia and Stax.

Aretha Franklin is often known as 'the Queen of Soul'.

Canadian-born country and western singer Shania Twain

COUNTRY MUSIC

Country, or country and western, music began as hillbilly music, the folk music of poor white Americans in rural areas of the southern states. Until the 1920s, it was played mostly at home, or at social occasions, on fiddles, guitars and banjos. Later, people began to play country music on electric instruments, such as electric guitars and keyboards. Record companies began to record it, and country music soon became a thriving commercial industry.

TRADITIONAL MUSIC

In many countries, traditional music is played at religious ceremonies, for work and for entertainment. Recently, some styles have been influenced by rock and pop. For instance, electric instruments are often used now alongside traditional ones.

Music to listen to

COUNTRY AND WESTERN
Hank Williams Sr., *20 Greatest Hits* (1998)
Patsy Cline, *Always* (1988)
Lyle Lovett, *Pontiac* (1988)

TRADITIONAL MUSIC
Ireland: Altan, *Island Angel* (1993)
The Rough Guide to World Music (1993, World Music Network)
Afro Celt Sound System, *Afro Celt Sound System Vol. 2* (1999)

ROCK AND ROLL
Bill Haley and the Comets, *Rock Around the Clock* (1955)
Elvis Presley, *Elvis Presley* (1956)
Buddy Holly, *The Chirping Crickets* (1957)

SOUL
Diana Ross and the Supremes, *40 Golden Motown Greats* (1998)
Marvin Gaye, *I Heard It Through The Grapevine* (1968)
Michael Jackson *Off The Wall* (1979)
Aretha Franklin *Lady soul* (1968)

MORE POPULAR STYLES

Kiss, a heavy metal group popular in the 70s and 80s, were famous for their outrageous clothes.

Music to listen to

BRITISH INVASION
The Beatles,
A Hard Day's Night
(1964)
The Rolling Stones,
Beggars Banquet
(1968)

ROCK
The Doors,
Strange Days
(1967)
The Who,
*The Who Sings
My Generation*
(1965)
Cream,
Disraeli Gears
(1967)

HEAVY METAL
Black Sabbath,
Paranoid (1971)
Led Zeppelin,
Led Zeppelin II
(1969)
Van Halen,
OU812 (1988)

REGGAE
Bob Marley,
Soul Rebels (1970)
Sly and Robbie,
Rhythm Killers
(1987)

BRITISH POP

The British invasion of pop began in the early 1960s when lots of British bands, starting with the Beatles, became very successful in the U.S. Their music was influenced by rock and roll, and other types of American pop.

ROCK

Rock first developed in the 1960s. It was different from rock and roll in that it usually relied on heavily amplified electric instruments. The music ranged from fairly simple ballads to songs that included complicated guitar solos. Rock was soon divided into lots of different categories, such as heavy metal and punk.

HEAVY METAL

Heavy metal usually features very loud amplified guitars and a heavy drum beat. It developed in the late 1960s from blues and R&B. This type of music is usually less tuneful than rock, with singers often screaming lyrics in between loud guitar chords.

REGGAE AND DUB

Reggae developed in Jamaica from R&B and different types of Caribbean popular music, such as styles called calypso and mento. In the late 1970s, record producers in Jamaica invented dub by editing out parts of reggae songs, then dropping them in again at different points in the song.

Bob Marley (1945-1981) is probably the most famous reggae singer in history.

PUNK

During the 70s, as unemployment and the outlook for young people in Britain got worse, the songs and extravagant lifestyles of rock stars became more and more irrelevant. The punk revolution was a move back to the basics of rock: music made by young people, expressing how they felt. The aggressive nature of the music was echoed in the punk image: unconventional clothes and a scowling expression.

Internet links

For links to websites where you can find sound and video clips from reggae, hip-hop and 1960s' British pop history, go to **www.usborne-quicklinks.com**

RAP AND HIP-HOP

In the late 70s, club DJs in New York began half-singing and half-talking over dance records. This is known as rap. The backing music for rap was made up of excerpts from other songs, called samples. The whole culture of rap, including the music and a type of dancing called break dancing, became known as hip-hop.

NEW ROMANTIC

In the UK, in the early 1980s, a cool and controlled style emerged in reaction to punk. The groups were called New Romantics. Bands such as Spandau Ballet used videos to help sell their music and their image.

HOUSE MUSIC

House is a type of dance music named after the Warehouse Club in Chicago where it first appeared in the 1980s. House usually has a strong bass line, often generated by a synthesizer, and a fast drum beat played on a drum machine. Similar types of music include techno, garage, and drum and bass.

Music to listen to

PUNK
The Clash,
Clash (1977)
The Ramones,
All the Stuff and More, Vol. 1 (1990)
The Buzzcocks,
Singles Going Steady (1979)

RAP
Grandmaster Flash,
Message from the Beat Street: The best of Grandmaster Flash (1994)
LL Cool J,
Mama said knock you out (1990)
Puff Daddy,
No Way Out (1997)

NEW ROMANTIC
Spandau Ballet,
Singles Collection (1985)
Duran Duran,
Duran Duran (1985)

HOUSE MUSIC
Soul II Soul,
Keep on Movin' (1989)
Various artists,
Vol. 1 - Best of House Music (1988)

Hip-hop star LL Cool J

THE MUSIC INDUSTRY

Music, especially rock music, is one of the biggest industries in the world. Songwriters, musicians and record companies all have the potential to make vast amounts of money when their music is played, and when CDs and tapes are sold. The musicians are what you see, but they are only a small part of the story. There is far more going on behind the scenes. The music industry provides a living for more agents, promoters and administrators than musicians.

RECORD COMPANIES

A few major record companies control most of the world market in recorded music. Giant companies such as Sony Music employ thousands of people. Smaller ones can't afford to spend as much on promotions as bigger ones. So, they often specialise in one particular kind of music. Below you can learn about the main departments in most record companies.

Internet link

For a link to a website where you can learn about jobs in the music industry and play music industry games, go to **www.usborne-quicklinks.com**

ARTIST AND REPERTOIRE (A&R) MANAGER

The A&R manager's job is to find performers to sign contracts with his or her record company. The manager usually goes to lots of gigs, and listens to demo tapes and CDs of new bands.

PUBLICITY DEPARTMENT

This department often starts publicising a band or album even before the band has started recording. Its most important job is to get bands mentioned in newspapers and magazines.

MARKETING DEPARTMENT

The marketing department is responsible for promoting a new band. It usually organizes advertisements in the press, posters and store display material before an album or single is released.

ART, OR CREATIVE, DEPARTMENT

This department designs album covers, video boxes and posters. Some record companies don't have their own art department, so they employ independent designers.

PRODUCTION DEPARTMENT

This department is in charge of getting CDs ready in time for the release date, which means having CD covers printed and the band's recordings copied.

SALES DEPARTMENT

The sales department is responsible for selling the albums themselves. Stores must receive CDs and tapes well before a release date, so they are ready to sell them on time.

PROMOTIONS DEPARTMENT

This department's job is to try to get singles played on radio and TV. This is a difficult task because hundreds of singles are released every week, but only a handful get to be played on air.

The art, or creative, department is in charge of designing album covers. Several different designs are usually put forward before one is chosen.

Tasco
BODY DOUBLE

Tasco
BODY DOUBLE

Tasco
BODY DOUBLE

MERCHANDISE

Some bands advertise themselves very well. After the release of their first album, *Spice,* in Britain in 1996, the Spice Girls became one of the world's most famous bands. They sold more merchandise, such as t-shirts and dolls, than most other bands. The all-girl band also signed deals with lots of different companies to advertise the Spice Girls' products. For example, by singing jingles and appearing on TV commercials.

A Spice Girls doll

T-shirts featuring the names or logos of famous bands are very popular.

SOUND RECORDING

Since people first began recording music in the late 1800s, the sound quality of recordings has improved enormously, from scratchy gramophone records to crystal-clear CDs. You can learn how sound is recorded on pages 60-61, but here you see what music has been recorded onto since the early 1900s.

Until the 1940s, people listened to music on records made from shellac, a brittle material that broke easily. They were played on a gramophone (top right).

In the late 1940s, shellac was replaced by vinylite, or vinyl, which is softer and more flexible, so it didn't break as easily.

Cassette tapes were developed in the U.S. in the early 1960s. For the first time, people could record music themselves on cassette.

From the 1980s, CDs gradually began to replace cassettes. The sound from CDs is much clearer than from records or tapes.

Mini Discs were introduced in 1992. They are like small CDs, but you can also record music onto a Mini Disc, like a cassette.

MP3 players were invented at the end of the 20th century. They allow you to store and listen to music from the Internet.

15

WHAT IS JAZZ?

One of the things that makes jazz different from classical music is that the musicians improvise, or make up, their own version of a tune, instead of playing notes that are written down by the composer. This means that players almost never perform a piece the same way twice.

Music to listen to

SAXOPHONE
Sonny Rollins,
The Sound of Sonny
(1957)
Clarence Clemons,
Rescue/Hero (1999)

CLARINET
Benny Goodman,
Live at Carnegie Hall 1938 (1950)

TRUMPET
Chet Baker,
'Round Midnight
(1998)

TROMBONE
Tommy Dorsey,
The 17 Number Ones (1990)

PIANO
Thelonius Monk,
Straight No Chaser
(1989)

DOUBLE BASS
Charlie Haden
Quartet West,
Now is the Hour
(1996)

DRUMS AND
VIBRAPHONE
Lionel Hampton,
Midnight Sun
(1993)

The saxophone is one of the most popular jazz instruments. Famous saxophone players include Sonny Rollins and Clarence Clemons.

HOW JAZZ MUSIC WORKS

Jazz is like a musical language. When the musicians play, it's as if they are talking to each other in jazz language.

Most jazz music is based on a tune or theme. The tune might be made up specially, or it might be based on a popular tune. A jazz group, or line-up, has two parts: the rhythm section and the front line.

THE FRONT LINE

Front line instruments are the ones that play solos during a jazz piece. They are given this name because the players usually stand in front of the rhythm section. Front line instruments include the clarinet, trombone, saxophone, trumpet and the right-hand side of a piano.

THE RHYTHM SECTION

The rhythm section is the part that keeps a steady pulse. It also plays the harmonies for the front line instruments to improvise over. Rhythm section instruments include the bass guitar, double bass, drums, and the left-hand side of a piano.

Jazz star Lionel Hampton plays drums and vibraphone, an instrument like a xylophone but with metal bars instead of wooden ones. The sound is amplified electronically.

RHYTHM AND SYNCOPATION

Most rhythms have a regular pulse, or beat. Normally, the stress, or accent, comes on the first beat in a bar. In jazz, the stress sometimes comes on the second beat, or in between the main beats. This is called syncopation. A tension is created between the steady pulse and the syncopated rhythm. See how this works in the diagrams on the right.

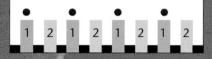

Here's a rhythm with 2 beats in each bar. The first beat of each bar is the strongest. This is shown by the red dots.

When the stress is on another beat of the bar, it is called syncopation. In the example above, the rhythm is syncopated because the stress is on the second beat. This is shown by the red dots on the second beat of each bar above.

JAM SESSIONS

When musicians get together without an audience and experiment with tunes, it is known as a jam session. It is during sessions like these that most jazz evolves.

Double bass player Charlie Haden is known for his experimental music.

Internet links

For links to websites where you can listen to jazz radio, read about famous jazz artists, and take an interactive class on the jazz legend Duke Ellington, go to **www.usborne-quicklinks.com**

COMPOSING JAZZ

Although jazz involves lots of improvisation, there are some fixed elements in a piece. Instead of writing down every note, jazz composers provide a rough outline, usually consisting of a tune and the chords that go with it. Chords are two or more notes played or sung together. They are usually written as chord symbols, which tell the musician which chords accompany a tune. The musicians improvise around this outline.

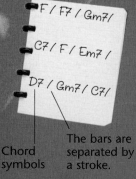

F / F7 / Gm7/
C7 / F / Em7 /
D7 / Gm7/ C7/

Chord symbols

The bars are separated by a stroke.

HOW JAZZ BEGAN

Music to listen to

DIXIELAND JAZZ
Louis Armstrong,
*Hot fives and sevens,
Box set* (1999)

Jelly Roll Morton,
*Jelly Roll Morton
(1923-1924)* (1992)

SWING
Billie Holiday,
*The Best of Billie
Holiday* (2000)

Glenn Miller,
*The Best of Glenn
Miller* (1939)

COOL JAZZ
Miles Davis,
Birth of the Cool
(1995)

At the end of the 19th century, the city of New Orleans was buzzing with the sounds of different types of music, as people from many parts of the world passed through its port. Some of these styles blended together to create a radically new kind of music. This became known as jazz.

The Paul Banks Orchestra, an early jazz band

THE ROOTS OF JAZZ

The origins of jazz lie mainly with African American music, such as blues and gospel. African American musicians began combining this music with some of the European styles around at the time, including French military band music, Spanish folk and European ballroom dance. Jazz was the result of this extraordinary mixture.

Early jazz tunes weren't written down, but were passed on by ear from one musician to another. In the 1920s, many jazz musicians went to look for work in cities such as Chicago. Their music became known as New Orleans or Dixieland jazz. Nowadays it is often called traditional or trad jazz.

Internet links

For links to websites where you can listen to different jazz styles and explore the roots of jazz in the US, with a clickable map and timeline, go to **www.usborne-quicklinks.com**

Billie Holiday (1915-1959), one of the greatest early jazz singers

SWING

In the 1930s, jazz bands got bigger so they could make an impact in huge ballrooms where people could dance to the music. The style of jazz they played was smoother and simpler than earlier jazz. It was known as swing, and the bands who played it were called swing bands, or big bands. Famous big bands include The Glen Miller Orchestra.

HOT AND COOL JAZZ

Some jazz musicians found swing dull, so they began to experiment with rhythm and harmony instead. The result was a loud, fiery, emotional style known as bebop, or modern jazz. Then, in the late 1940s, the cool school developed. Cool jazz was much gentler, more laid-back and less emotional than modern jazz.

THE 1950s AND AFTER

In the 1950s, a style known as West Coast jazz took root in California. This was far more relaxed than bebop. Then came a much freer style, called free jazz, which ignored all the rules about harmony and structure.

LOUIS ARMSTRONG (1900-1971)

Louis Armstrong was such a brilliant cornet player that he had a radical effect on the future of jazz. Before he came on the scene, it was usual for bands to play together most of the time. But Louis was so good that his band let him play many of the pieces on his own. Solos have played a major part in jazz ever since.

MUSIC IN ANCIENT TIMES

An Egyptian tomb painting showing a harp player and a dancer

People have been making music ever since they began trying to communicate with each other. Even before there were proper musical instruments, people made sounds with their voices, or by clapping and hitting things. We know about these activities from pictures discovered in ancient caves, as early civilizations hadn't yet learned any form of writing.

EGYPTIAN MUSIC

Over 3,000 years ago, in ancient Egypt, music is thought to have played a large part in everyday life. Dancers and flute players often accompanied work, such as planting crops, while other musicians entertained kings and noblemen at court. Music was also very important in Egyptian religious ceremonies, and some people studied it in special colleges.

ROMAN MUSIC

In ancient Rome, music was used to accompany entertainers, such as jugglers and acrobats, and parts of plays were often set to music. Most musicians were slaves, but some rich people learned to play too. They didn't play in public though, as this was felt to be undignified.

This mosaic, showing Roman street musicians, dates from around the 1st century B.C.

GREEK MUSIC

The word 'music' comes from an old Greek word, *mousike*, named after the muses, who were the goddesses of art and science. Music was regarded so highly in ancient Greece that people thought it was the invention of the gods.

MEDIEVAL MUSIC

In the Middle Ages in Europe, from around 500 to 1500, music played a central part in Christian worship. Church services were all sung, rather than spoken.

CHURCH MUSIC

In early Medieval times, religious music consisted of a single tune with no harmonies. This is called plainsong, or plainchant. From about 800, monks began to sing a drone (a continuous note) to accompany the tune. By the end of the 12th century, two or more lines of melody were being sung at the same time. This is known as polyphony.

MUSIC FOR ENTERTAINMENT

From around 900, musicians known as *jongleurs* went from village to village, or castle to castle, earning a living by playing, singing and performing tricks. There were also male poets and composers who performed for wealthy people. They were often noblemen themselves, and they usually sang simple love songs. In France, they were known as *troubadours* and *trouvères*, and in Germany, as *Minnesingers*.

This picture, from around 1300, shows musicians entertaining at court.

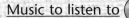

Music to listen to

MEDIEVAL MUSIC FOR ENTERTAINMENT
Ensemble Unicorn, *Early Music - Music of the Troubadours* (1998)
Ensemble Lucidarium, *Troubadours and Minnesänger* (1998)

MEDIEVAL CHURCH MUSIC
Musique D'abord, *Medieval English Music* (1997)

Medieval musicians playing a lute, a small harp and a pair of instruments called a pipe and tabor. A pipe is played with one hand while the other hand beats a drum.

Internet links

For links to websites where you can listen to Medieval and Ancient Greek music, go to **www.usborne-quicklinks.com**

RENAISSANCE MUSIC

In Italy, in the 14th century, new ideas about art and learning began to form, inspired by the culture of ancient Greece and Rome, stimulating changes which marked the end of the Middle Ages and the beginning of modern times. Over the next 200 years, these ideas influenced all of Europe. This period is called the Renaissance, meaning 'rebirth'.

Two popular Renaissance instruments were the harp (left) and a type of organ called a portative organ (right).

RENAISSANCE INSTRUMENTS

People often played or sang, or both, in small groups called consorts. Often, they played sets of the same instrument, each at a different pitch. The lute was a popular Renaissance instrument. Others included wind instruments, such as the shawm and crumhorn.

INSTRUMENTAL MUSIC

Before this period, instruments were mainly used simply to accompany singers and dancers. But, during the 1500s, composers began to write instrumental music for its own sake. Many of these composers began to work at the courts of wealthy noblemen, writing music for their entertainment.

This group, featuring a flute, a lute and a singer, is performing a song by a French composer Claudin de Sermisy (1490-1562).

Music to listen to

CHURCH MUSIC
Tallis Scholars, *The Best of the Renaissance* (1999)

INSTRUMENTAL MUSIC
Piffaro, *A Flemish Feast - Flemish Renaissance Wind Music* (2000)
Rose Consort of Viols with Red Byrd, *Orlando Gibbons: Consort and keyboard music, Songs and Anthems* (1994)

MADRIGALS
Hallé Madrigal Singers, *La Bella Ninfa* (1998)

This early 16th century print shows a printing press at work.

THE INVENTION OF PRINTING

One of the most significant changes of this time was the invention of printing in the mid-1500s. It played a huge part in spreading new ideas about art and music. Before this, books had to be written out by hand, which made them a rare and expensive luxury. Now they could be copied quickly and cheaply.

The first book of music was printed in Italy, but soon, music was being printed all over Europe. More people learned to read music and play instruments. So many composers began to write simple, popular music for amateurs to play.

Internet links

For links to websites where you can listen to Renaissance music and hear how some early instruments sounded, go to **www.usborne-quicklinks.com**

MADRIGALS

Small groups often gathered together to sing songs called madrigals. These were written for up to six voices, and each part had its own melody line. Madrigals were first written in Italy in the early 14th century, but they soon became popular throughout Europe. The words were often about the problems of love.

RELIGIOUS MUSIC

In the Middle Ages, the Roman Catholic Church had been the main religion in Europe. But in the 16th century, some people, known as Protestants, began to break away and set up their own churches.

Catholic services had been sung in Latin (the official language of the Church) by a choir of monks, but the music for Protestant services was designed for the congregation to sing. The music itself was much simpler and the words were written in the people's own languages. The idea of the congregation singing soon became popular all over northern Europe.

Characters in religious paintings, like this angel, were often shown playing instruments.

WRITING MUSIC DOWN

Before the invention of sound recording, the only way to describe music, without actually singing or playing it, was to find a way of writing it down. This is called music notation. Over the years, people developed different ways of doing this. The system of notation described on the opposite page took hundreds of years to develop.

EARLY NOTATION

The first known attempts at writing music down date back to the 7th century. People drew dots, lines and curves to show roughly where the tune got higher or lower. But these signs, called neumes, did not show the exact pitch or length of each note. So they only worked as a reminder to musicians of music they had already learned.

This 11th century manuscript was written in Italy. The symbols written over the words showed singers roughly what to sing.

A NEW TYPE OF NOTATION

At the beginning of the 11th century, an Italian monk named Guido d'Arezzo developed a better way of notating music. He used a set of lines, called a staff, or stave, to show the pitch of the notes. At first, notes were written as solid diamonds or rectangles. The way the notes were grouped together, and how far apart they were, gave musicians a general idea of how long each note lasted.

This Medieval manuscript of religious music shows musical notes as black diamonds and rectangles, written on red four-line staves.

Gradually, people began to use different kinds of oval noteheads to show the exact length of each note. By around the 16th century, a music notation system had been established that was similar to the one we use today.

MODERN MUSIC NOTATION

Musical notes are written on a set of five lines called a staff (or stave). Each note name has a different position on the staff. The position varies according to a sign called a clef. There are different types of clef, but in keyboard music there are two: treble and bass. The treble clef is normally used for high notes, and the bass clef for low notes. The higher the pitch of a note, the higher up the staff it is written. Below you can see how the notes on the staff correspond to the keys on a keyboard.

Piano or keyboard music uses two staves, written one above the other. Usually, the top staff is for right-hand notes written in the treble clef, and the bottom staff is for left-hand notes written in the bass clef. But both hands can play notes on either staff, and both staves can use either clef.

On the staff, notes are written on the lines and in the spaces between the lines.

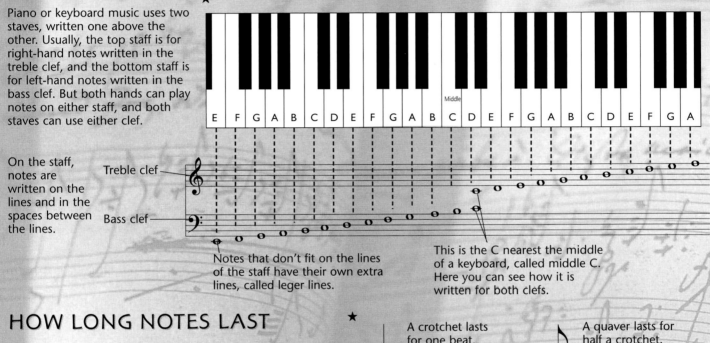

Treble clef

Bass clef

Notes that don't fit on the lines of the staff have their own extra lines, called leger lines.

This is the C nearest the middle of a keyboard, called middle C. Here you can see how it is written for both clefs.

HOW LONG NOTES LAST

As well as showing you the pitch of each note, music notation shows you how long to make each one last. Note-lengths are measured in steady counts called beats. The shape of a note shows how many beats it lasts for. On the right are some of the most common note lengths.

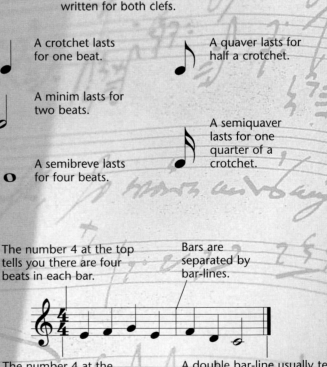

A crotchet lasts for one beat.

A minim lasts for two beats.

A semibreve lasts for four beats.

A quaver lasts for half a crotchet.

A semiquaver lasts for one quarter of a crotchet.

GROUPING NOTES TOGETHER

When music is written down, it is split into sections called bars by vertical lines called bar-lines. Each bar contains the same number of beats. At the beginning of the staff, a sign called a time signature shows how many beats there are in each bar, and what kind of beats they are. On the right, you can see an example of a time signature called four-four time.

The number 4 at the top tells you there are four beats in each bar.

Bars are separated by bar-lines.

The number 4 at the bottom tells you they are crotchet beats.

A double bar-line usually tells you that you have reached the end of the music.

25

SCALES

Most musical compositions are based on a scale. A scale is a set of notes going up and down the staff. There are lots of different types of scales, and the type used affects the sound of the music. If music from another part of the world sounds very different from the music you are used to, it could be because it is based on a different sort of scale.

This is Vanessa Mae, a virtuoso classical violinist. Lots of classical musicians play scales as part of their practice.

INTERVALS

The difference in pitch between two notes is called an interval. For instance, on a piano, the smallest interval is between one key and the next one immediately to the left or right of it, with no keys in between. This interval is called a semitone.

Two semitones make one tone. On a keyboard, a tone is the distance between two keys when there is one key in between. Below, you can see which pairs of keys are a semitone apart and which are a tone apart.

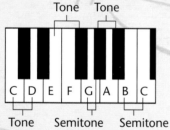

Tone   Tone

C D E F G A B C

Tone   Semitone   Semitone

OTHER TYPES OF INTERVALS

Some music, including certain types of Indian music, uses intervals smaller than a semitone. This means that it cannot be written on a staff. It is usually memorised, or improvised around memorised patterns of notes, although some music specialists have developed ways of writing it down.

An Indian musician playing a snake flute, called a been.

SCALE NAMES

Each scale is named after the note on which it begins. It usually finishes on the next note with the same name. The interval between the two is called an octave.

MAJOR AND MINOR SCALES

Since about 1600, most Western music has been based on major and minor scales. Major scales have a different pattern of tones and semitones from minor scales. This makes them sound quite different from each other.

The simplest type of major scale you can play on a piano or keyboard starts on the note C and uses only the white notes. Below, you can see the pattern of tones and semitones in the scale of C major. You can find out about minor scales on page 79.

★   T = tone   S = semitone

T T S T T T S

A tune based around the scale of C major is said to be in the key of C major.

MODES

Medieval and Renaissance music, as well as some Western traditional music, is based on ancient scales called modes. Modes were first used in Medieval times, but they have Greek names because the people who named them were very influenced by ancient Greek writers on music. Each mode begins on a different note and, on a keyboard, the modes use the white keys only. Try playing the modes on the right and see how the patterns of tones and semitones make each one sound different.

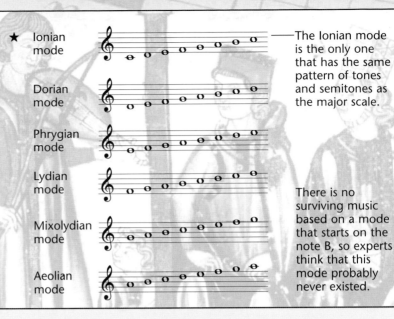

★ Ionian mode

Dorian mode

Phrygian mode

Lydian mode

Mixolydian mode

Aeolian mode

The Ionian mode is the only one that has the same pattern of tones and semitones as the major scale.

There is no surviving music based on a mode that starts on the note B, so experts think that this mode probably never existed.

MORE SCALES

If you have a piano or keyboard, you could try playing some of the different types of scale below. Listen to how different they sound from C major.

PENTATONIC SCALE

A pentatonic scale is made up of five notes, followed by the note an octave apart from the first note. Lots of traditional music from China and Japan is based on pentatonic scales.

The black keys on a keyboard form a Chinese pentatonic scale. So do the keys marked by the red dots on the left.

CHROMATIC SCALE

A chromatic scale includes all 12 black and white keys between two notes with the same name. It is a sequence of 12 semitones.

WHOLE-TONE SCALE

A whole-tone scale has six equal steps of a tone each.

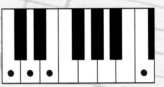

Some 20th century composers based their music on chromatic and whole-tone scales.

This instrument, a shamisen, is used for different types of Japanese music, lots of which is based on pentatonic scales.

BAROQUE MUSIC

The name Baroque describes a highly ornamental style of European art, architecture and music from around 1600 to 1750. Baroque paintings and buildings were very ornate, and the music echoed this. Many new musical forms developed at this time, including opera and new instrumental music, such as the suite, concerto and sonata.

HARMONY

Before this period, the main style of music was polyphony, in which several lines of melody were played at the same time. From around 1600, music began to consist of one main tune, accompanied by low-sounding bass parts, and chords (one or more notes played together), played on a keyboard instrument such as a harpsichord or organ. This is known as the *basso continuo* part.

Most composers didn't write out the chords in full. Instead, the keyboard music consisted of the bass part with numbers written on it. The musician played chords shown by the numbers. This is called figured bass. The chords acted as a framework, which players improvised around. For example, they might make up melodies to go with the chords.

An example of figured bass

PUBLIC CONCERTS

Most composers were employed by wealthy people or the church, to write music for religious sevices and for entertainment at court. Public concerts, where the audience payed to see a performance, began in the late 1600s. This meant that composers could now write music to suit the tastes of a much wider audience, rather than just the church or nobility.

Handel made a living mostly from staging his operas and religious works called oratorios.

A Baroque harpsichord

Pressing a key on a harpsichord causes a string to be plucked by a plectrum. This is what makes the sound.

ORCHESTRAS

The orchestra, as we know it today, began in the 1600s. The first orchestras were very haphazard, and composers included whatever instruments and players were available. There were usually violins though, as well as cellos or bassoons, and a harpsichord or organ to play the basso continuo part. There could also be violas, oboes, horns, trumpets and drums.

NEW TYPES OF MUSIC

Baroque composers began to write longer works for instruments than ever before. They structured them in different ways. As a result, new forms developed, such as the suite, concerto and sonata. Instruments also improved in the Baroque. For instance, keys were added to flutes, so more notes could be played.

A Baroque flute with one key

THE SUITE

A suite is a collection of instrumental pieces, usually dance tunes, designed to be played one after the other. Baroque suites were written for solo instruments, such as the harpsichord or flute, as well as orchestra. They were not actually meant for dancing to, just for listening to, but their style and rhythm was based on Baroque dances.

CONCERTOS AND SONATAS

Two types of concertos were popular in the Baroque. The *concerto grosso* was for a small group of instruments and an orchestra. Sometimes the small group played alone, and sometimes it played with the orchestra, but they both played similar music. The solo concerto was an orchestral piece with one or two soloists. The soloist's music was usually quite different to that of the orchestra.

The trio sonata is a piece in a few sections, or movements, for one or two instruments with basso continuo. After 1700, solo sonatas for one instrument and continuo became more popular.

Internet link

For a link to a website with an online guide to Baroque music and sound clips to listen to, go to **www.usborne-quicklinks.com**

This is the cello part from a solo concerto by Vivaldi, which was published around 1711.

Music to listen to

SUITE
Rameau, Harpsichord suites
Bach, Orchestral suite, no. 1

CONCERTO GROSSO
Corelli, Concerto grosso, op. 6, no. 2

SOLO CONCERTO
Vivaldi, Op. 8, nos 1-4, 'The Four Seasons'

This painting, from around 1690, shows Baroque musicians playing at court.

Cello

A plucked stringed instrument called a mandolin

An early viola called a *viola di brazzo*

Harpsichord

Violin

CLASSICAL MUSIC

Around 1750, a lighter, more graceful style of music began to replace the intricacy and grandeur of the Baroque. Musicians use the term 'Classical' (with a capital C) for music written from around 1750 to 1820. It was during this period that the structures of many types of music were established.

A manuscript by Mozart, one of the most influential Classical composers.

TYPE OF PIECE	MOVEMENTS	INSTRUMENTS
Symphony	3 – 4	Orchestra
Concerto	3	Orchestra with one or more soloists
Overture	1	Orchestra
Sonata	1 – 4	1 or 2
String quartet	4	4 solo stringed instruments: 2 violins, viola and cello

Here you can see the structures of some musical forms that were established during the Classical period, and the instruments used in each one.

CLASSICAL ORCHESTRAL MUSIC

By around the middle of the 18th century, orchestras had developed much the same layout as they have today, but they were much smaller. Early Classical composers no longer wrote figured basses, as Baroque composers had done, but they still used a keyboard instrument to play chords and make the music sound fuller.

THE SYMPHONY

A large-scale work for orchestra, called the symphony, first appeared early in the Classical period. The first symphonies were usually in three movements, but four soon became standard. The word 'symphony' came from *sinfonia*, a term which had been used to decribe several different types of Renaissance and Baroque instrumental music.

THE CONCERTO

The Classical concerto grew out of the Baroque solo concerto. It is a work for one or more soloists and orchestra, usually in three movements. A concerto shows off a soloist's skill. Towards the end of a movement, the soloist often plays a difficult passage. This is called a *cadenza* and it is the soloist's chance to end with a flourish.

Internet links

For links to websites where you can find an interactive symphony adventure, discover more about chamber music, and find out about Mozart's fascinating life, go to **www.usborne-quicklinks.com**

THE OVERTURE

An overture is a piece for orchestra, usually in a single movement. Overtures were first written during early Baroque times to let the audience know that an opera was about to begin. They were also written to introduce other large-scale works, including oratorios. Classical composers such as Mozart began to link the opera overture to the opera itself, by using some of the same melodies, or themes.

THE CLASSICAL SONATA

The Classical sonata contained some elements of both the Baroque trio and solo sonatas. It was still in several movements, and at least one was usually a dance, such as a minuet. Sonatas were written for one or two instruments alone: such as piano, or violin and keyboard (which, before the electronic keyboard, meant harpsichord, organ or piano).

The piano began to replace the harpsichord around this time, and composers began to write more sonatas for piano alone. Mozart himself wrote 32. Some were for his pupils; others were more difficult and were designed to show off his own keyboard skills at concerts.

In this picture, Haydn (right) is leading a string quartet. The string quartet (2 violins, vlola and cello) was a very popular Classical form.

CHAMBER MUSIC

Chamber music is written for a group of solo players. From around the beginning of the Classical period, the name was given to music that is suitable for performance in a chamber, or room, even though composers had been writing music for small groups of musicians for hundreds of years. In the past, it was played in the homes of noblemen, but today it is usually played in concert halls.

The title of a piece of chamber music varies according to the number of instruments in the piece. For example, a quartet always has four players, a trio has three players, and so on.

Music to listen to

ORCHESTRAL MUSIC
Haydn, Surprise Symphony no. 94 in G Major; Trumpet Concerto in E Flat
Mozart, Overture to *The Magic Flute*; Piano Sonata no. 11 in A Major
Beethoven, Symphony no. 5; Violin Concerto in D, op. 61

CHAMBER MUSIC
Haydn, Quartet in C, op. 76, no. 3 (Emperor Quartet)
Mozart, Oboe Quartet in F Major
Beethoven, Archduke Trio in B flat, op. 97

The viola sounds lower than the violin.

Violin

The cello plays the lowest notes.

Haydn Is playing one of the violin parts.

ROMANTIC MUSIC

A new style of music became fashionable in 19th century Europe, that was inspired by nature and other arts, such as poetry and painting. Composers, as well as painters and writers, tried to use their art to express feelings and emotions. This movement in the arts is known as Romanticism, and it lasted until the early 1900s.

Composers such as Mahler and Mendelssohn began to write symphonies and concertos on a much bigger scale, and some others began using music to express national identity. This was also the time when lots of the most famous operas and ballets were written. You can find out more about these later in the book.

THE FIRST ROMANTIC

Although Beethoven wrote most of his music during the Classical era, he is thought to be the first Romantic composer. He developed a new musical style that was more complicated than anything written before. He had a huge influence on later 19th century music although, during his lifetime, some people found his music too complex and difficult.

ROMANTIC ORCHESTRAS

In the 1800s, new instruments, such as the cor anglais, were added to the orchestra, and some existing ones, such as the trumpet, were improved. 19th century orchestras were also bigger than ever before.

The cor anglais, added to the orchestra in the 19th century

TELLING A STORY

Some 19th century composers wrote descriptive music to tell a story. One example of this is called a symphonic, or tone, poem. Composers created atmosphere by their use of rhythm, harmony, *tempo* (speed) and their choice of instruments. For example, rapid or unexpected changes of key were used to create a feeling of suspense or turmoil.

Beethoven is often considered to be one of the most important composers in history.

Internet links

For links to websites where you can listen to radio shows about Beethoven, Schubert and other Romantic composers, and hear their music, go to
www.usborne-quicklinks.com

ROMANTIC SONGS AND PIANO MUSIC

A performance of *Winterreise*, a song cycle (set of songs) by Schubert.

The word *Lied* means 'song' in German, but it usually applies to a particular type of 19th century song, written for a solo singer and piano. Schubert was the first important composer of *Lieder**: he wrote over 600 of them.

The piano was probably the most popular 19th century instrument. Composers such as Chopin wrote piano pieces that expressed a particular mood. His *Nocturnes*, for example, suggest nighttime, and are quiet and peaceful in character.

GREAT VIRTUOSOS

Some 19th century musicians became very famous. Brilliant instrumentalists, or virtuosos, such as the violinist Nicolò Paganini, had lots of fans and were the equivalent of today's pop stars. Many composers wrote very difficult music specially for them.

AMATEUR MUSICIANS

Many 19th century composers also wrote much simpler music for amateur musicians to play. This was played mostly for pleasure by local groups of musicians and singers, or by families at home. Family music-making was very popular in the 19th and early 20th centuries, before recorded music was available to listen to.

A caricature of the virtuoso violinist, Nicolò Paganini (1782-1840)

* '*Lieder*' is the plural of '*Lied*'.

NATIONALIST MUSIC

Before the 19th century, European music had been dominated by certain Western countries: Italy in the Baroque period, then Germany and France in the Classical era. Some Romantic composers, especially in Russia and Eastern Europe, rebelled against this and tried to express their own national identity in their music. This became known as the Nationalist movement in music.

These are Russian musicians playing an accordion (left) and balalaika, which are traditional Russian instruments.

The Spanish composer Manuel de Falla was very influenced by the music of his native country. Here you can see a Spanish flamenco dancer accompanied by a guitar.

RUSSIA

Around the middle of the 19th century, a group of five Russian composers decided to concentrate on writing music which sounded unmistakeably Russian. The music they wrote was based on the folk music and dances of their country. This group became known as 'The Russian Five' or 'The Mighty Handful'.

Operas written by members of the group were especially successful, in other parts of Europe as well as in Russia. At this time, the fashionable language for opera was Italian, but operas by members of 'The Five' were sung in Russian. One of the most famous of their operas is *Boris Godunov* by Musorgsky.

Tchaikovsky (1840-1893), another Russian composer, had been successfully writing music in a Western European style. But he was so impressed by the music of 'The Russian Five', that he decided to try to make his own music sound more Russian. When he combined his style with folk tunes, his music became more popular than ever before.

Musorgsky (1839-1881) of 'The Russian Five'

BOHEMIA

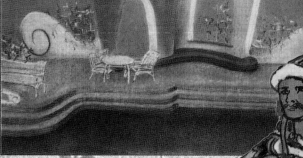

Scenery for *The Two Widows*, an opera by the Bohemian composer Smetana

A costume design from another Smetana opera called *Libuse*

In the early 1800s, the Czech province of Bohemia was part of the Austro-Hungarian empire. Children were not even taught their own language in schools. Around 1850, however, there was a movement to revive the Czech language and culture. Some composers expressed their feelings by returning to traditional styles of Bohemian music. When Smetana, a Czech composer, returned to his native Bohemia after living in Western Europe, he began to learn to speak Czech for the first time. He then based most of his music on Czech folk tunes and legends.

Internet link

For a link to a website where you can listen to the music of some Nationalist composers, go to **www.usborne-quicklinks.com**

The 20th century was a time of experimentation. Many composers reacted against the lavishness of Romanticism and chose to strike out in new directions. This led to a fascinating variety of new sounds and techniques.

EXPERIMENTS WITH KEY

Since the Renaissance, most Western music has been in a particular key. This is called tonal music. Some 20th century composers began to experiment with bitonal music, music written in two keys at once. Others wrote atonal music: music that isn't in any key at all. This experimentation with keys makes some 20th century music sounds harsh and odd.

THE IMPRESSIONISTS

Impressionist music takes its name from the Impressionist movement in art. Impressionist artists conveyed the impact of a scene using lighting effects, rather than painting realistically. In the same way, Impressionist composers tried to conjure up sensations through music. Debussy used chords and instruments for their sound quality, rather than obeying any traditional musical rules.

Internet links

For links to websites with music by Debussy, Philip Glass and other 20th century composers, go to **www.usborne-quicklinks.com**

NEO-CLASSICAL MUSIC

Neo means 'new' or 'modernised'. From about 1920, composers such as Stravinsky began to reject Romanticism. Instead of composing for huge orchestras in a weighty Romantic style, composers wrote for smaller groups. They combined musical forms from earlier periods with modern trends, including the use of atonal harmonies.

Music to listen to

IMPRESSIONIST MUSIC
Debussy, *Prélude à L'après Midi d'un Faune*

SERIAL MUSIC
Schoenberg, String quartet no. 3

NEO-CLASSICAL MUSIC
Stravinsky, *Pulcinella; The Rake's Progress*

ALEATORY MUSIC
John Cage, *Music of changes; Imaginary Landscape no. 4*

MINIMAL MUSIC
Philip Glass, *Satyagraha*

MUSIQUE CONCRÈTE
Pierre Henry, *La Messe de Liverpool*

ELECTRONIC MUSIC
Stockhausen, *Gesang der Jünglinge; Telemusik*

A character from an opera by Debussy called *Pelléas et Mélisande*

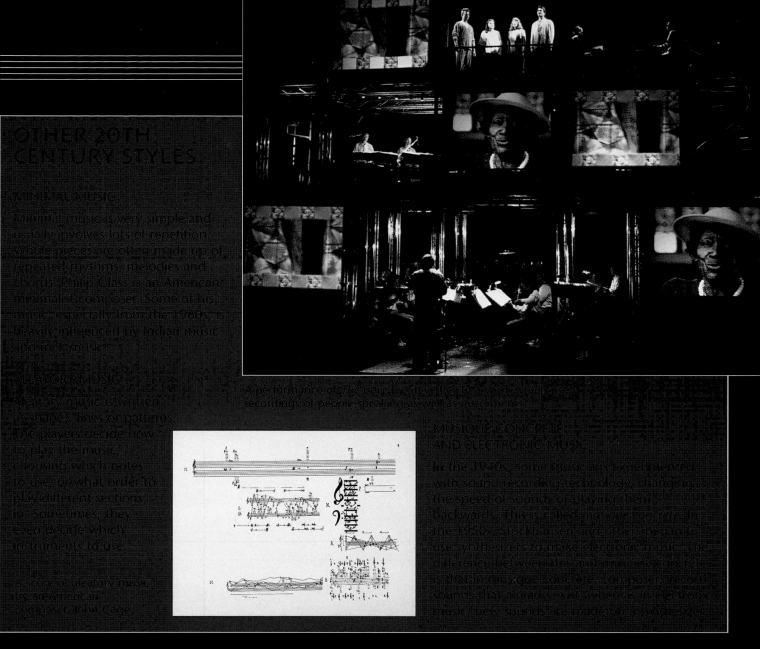

OTHER 20TH CENTURY STYLES

MINIMAL MUSIC

Minimal music is very simple and usually involves lots of repetition. Whole pieces are often made up of repeated rhythms, melodies and chords. Philip Glass is an American minimalist composer. Some of his music, especially from the 1960s, is heavily influenced by Indian music and rock music.

ALEATORY MUSIC

Aleatory music is written as shapes, lines or patterns. The players decide how to play the music, choosing which notes to use, or what order to play different sections in. Sometimes, they even decide which instruments to use.

A score of aleatory music by an American composer, John Cage.

A performance of *The Cave* by Steve Reich, a work which uses recordings of people speaking as well as instruments.

MUSIQUE CONCRÈTE AND ELECTRONIC MUSIC

In the 1940s, some musicians experimented with sound recording technology, changing the speed of sounds or playing them backwards. This is called *musique concrète*. In the 1950s, Stockhausen and others began to use synthesizers to make electronic music. The difference between this and musique concrète is that in musique concrète, composers record sounds that already exist, whereas in electronic music, new sounds are made on a synthesizer.

SERIAL MUSIC

In the early 20th century, Schoenberg and his pupils, Berg and Webern, invented a new way of writing music. They started to base their music on the chromatic scale (see page 27). This became known as serial, or 12-note, music.

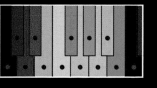

This is what a chromatic scale looks like on a keyboard.

The composer makes a pattern of notes using each note in the chromatic scale once. The pattern is called a note row, or tone row. The row is then repeated in different ways to create a piece of music. There are some examples on the right.

Note row:

Note row played backwards:

Note row shared between two instruments:

The lengths of the notes in the note row are changed:

MUSIC IN THE FAR EAST

Traditional
music from
the Far East sounds very
different from Western music. This
is partly due to the types of instruments
that are played, but it is mainly because
music from this part of the world is
based on different types of intervals,
scales and rhythms.

Internet links

For links to websites where you can listen to music and
instruments of the Far East, create your own bhangra
mix online and play along with a gamelan, go to
www.usborne-quicklinks.com

CHINA

In the late 1700s, a type of opera developed in
China called Beijing, or Peking, opera. As well as
singing, it includes dancing and acrobatics. The
costumes are very elaborate, and the performers
wear masks or bright makeup.

JAPAN

The koto is one of
the oldest Japanese
instruments. It is
played by pressing
strings with one
hand while plucking
them with the other.

The strings on a koto
are stretched over a
wooden frame, on
which there are small,
moveable pieces of
wood called bridges.

In Beijing opera,
different meanings are
conveyed by gestures
made with the
singers' hands
and feet.

INDIA

Indian music is traditionally not written down. Instead, musicians learn patterns of notes, called *ragas*, and rhythms called *talas*, and they improvise around them. There are hundreds of ragas, each designed for a different season or time of day. The musicians try to create a certain mood through the music.

BHANGRA MUSIC

Bhangra was originally the name for the traditional music of Punjab, a region of northern India and Pakistan. In this sort of music, a singer is accompanied by traditional drums. Bhangra is now also the name for a popular style of dance music that was first played in the UK. It is a combination of Punjabi folk music, and different types of popular dance music, such as hip-hop and house. Modern bhangra music combines traditional Punjabi instruments with

Apache Indian, a very successful British bhangra star

electronic instruments such as synthesizers and drum machines.

From the 1950s, lots of people from Punjab emigrated to the UK, bringing their music with them. By the early 1980s, bhangra had developed into the infectious dance music that has become so popular.

Music to listen to

CHINA
Peking Opera: The Forest on Fire (1995)

JAPAN
Koto Music of Japan (1993, Laserlight)

INDIA
Ustad Imrat Khan, *Indian Music for Sitar and Surba* (1992)

BHANGRA MUSIC
Apache Indian, *Make Way for the Indian* (1995)

INDONESIA
Various artists, *Gamelan Music of Bali* (1997, Lyrichord)

INDONESIA

Indonesian orchestras are called gamelans and are made up of different types of percussion instruments, such as drums and gongs. They also use metallophones, which are like xylophones but with metal bars instead of wooden ones. Every Indonesian town or village usually has its own gamelan. The instruments are all made locally, so each has an individual sound. Musicians improvise around two five-note, or pentatonic, scales.

This Gamelan is from the Indonesian island of Bali.

MUSIC IN AFRICA

Home to hundreds of millions of people, there are around 1,000 different languages spoken in Africa. This cultural variety is reflected in the nation's music, making the continent one of the most musically diverse regions in the world. These two pages deal with the music of Africa south of the Sahara Desert. The music of North Africa is covered under 'Arab music' on page 43.

RHYTHM AND MELODY

In African music, rhythm is often the most important feature. There is a wide range of percussion instruments, and singers and melody instruments are often used to provide a rhythm instead of a tune. For example, stringed instruments are sometimes plucked or struck.

African and Western music use similar intervals and scales, so people in the West usually find it easier to listen to than music from, say, China or Japan. Melodies are based on short phrases which the players improvise around. The melodies are simple, but the rhythms are complex.

This Namibian dancer is singing and clapping her hands as she dances.

This instrument is called a musical bow. It is played by striking the string with a stick. The player's mouth acts as a resonator.

SINGING

Traditional African songs often involve a solo singer, who acts as a leader, along with a chorus. The songs are usually passed on from one generation to the other, rather than being written down.

This group, called the Drummers of Burundi, do concerts all round the world.

AFRICAN DRUMS

African drums come in different shapes and sizes, but most are made from hollowed logs and animal skins. They are sometimes played in large groups, led by a master drummer.

AFRICAN POPULAR MUSIC

In recent decades, traditional African music has been overshadowed by new forms of African popular music. Most of these styles combine elements from Western popular music with elements from traditional African music. One popular style from Nigeria is called juju. It uses traditional Nigerian rhythms, but it is played on Western instruments such as electric guitars. Another popular style is highlife from Ghana and Nigeria.

Internet links

For links to websites where you can listen to different types of music from all over Africa and explore Nigerian culture, go to **www.usborne-quicklinks.com**

King Sunny Ade, sometimes called the 'Minister of enjoyment', is one of the most famous juju stars.

Music to listen to

Various artists, *African Tribal Music and Dances (Box set)* (1995, Laserlight)
Various artists, *Kings of African Music* (1997, Music Club)
Various artists, *Ghana, Ancient Ceremonies* (1991, Nonesuch)
The Drummers of Burundi, *The Drummers of Burundi, Live at the Real World* (1993)
Ndere Troupe, *Ngoma, Music from Uganda* (1997)
Various artists, *African Highlife Vol. 1: Soukous/Mbalax* (1998)

NATIVE AMERICAN MUSIC

There are hundreds of different tribes of Native Americans, each with their own customs and traditions. But their music has much in common. For instance, singing is the most popular form of music-making, especially among tribes in North America.

Native North American drums

Music to listen to

NATIVE NORTH AMERICAN
Various artists, *Authentic Native American Music* (1995)
R. Carlos Nakai, *Changes: Native American Flute Music* (1992)

SOUTH AMERICAN
Various artists, *Bolivia, Charangos & Guitarrillas* (1996)

Native American dancers often wear bells around their legs and shake rattles as they dance.

SONGS

Most North American songs are based around simple melodies, sung in a high-sounding, strained voice. During a song, people often add grunts, whistles and hisses. This is known as 'mouth music' and it adds rhythm and contrast to the rest of the music. Songs are usually also accompanied by drums and rattles.

INSTRUMENTS

Native North Americans use very few instruments. The ones that are used, mostly drums, flutes and rattles, are mainly only used to accompany singing. Native South Americans have a much wider range of instruments. In particular, they have a range of pipes, made of reeds, wood and clay.

A South American musician playing the panpipes and a drum

In some parts of America, people alter or amplify their voices, using trumpets made of bark or bamboo.

CEREMONIES

Music plays a very important role in Native American gatherings, or powwows, and ceremonies. At these ceremonies, ancient dances are performed alongside people chanting and beating drums.

ARAB MUSIC

Although the music varies from region to region, traditional Arab music is played all over the Arab-speaking world: in North Africa, as well as the Middle East. In the Arab world, music and dancing are very much social activities. Music isn't used very much in Islam, the main Arab religion, except for chanting prayers.

Drummers and flute players from Morocco in North Africa

THE MUSIC

Singing is probably the most popular type of music-making. Accompanying instruments usually play the same melody as the singer. Songs are based on scales called modes, which sound very different from Western modes.

Musicians also improvise around sets of rhythm patterns called rhythmic modes.

The European lute, shown here, was brought to Europe in the Middle Ages from the Middle East where it is known as an ud.

ARAB INSTRUMENTS

Two of the most common stringed instruments in Arab music are the ud and the rabab. The rabab is like a fiddle, but it has a spike at the end of it, which rests on the ground as it is being played.

Internet links

For links to websites where you can watch video clips of pow-wows and listen to Native American and Arab music, go to **www.usborne-quicklinks.com**

Music to listen to

Various artists, *The Music of Islam* (1997, Celestial Harmonies); George Mgrdichian, *Now Sounds of the Middle East* (1996) Hamza Shakkur, *World Network Vol. 27: Syria: Takasim & Sufi Chants* (1994)

THE SCIENCE OF SOUND

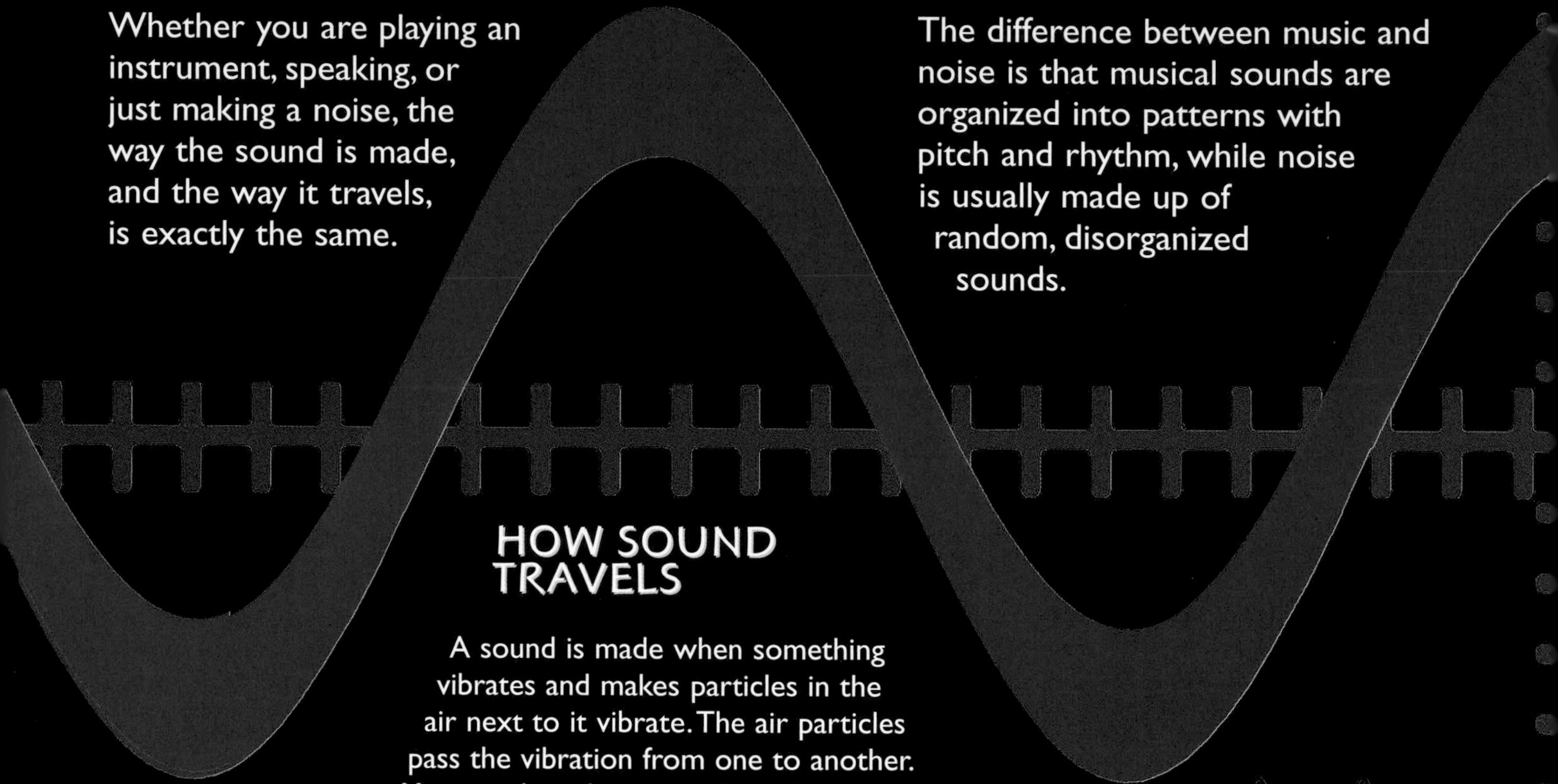

Whether you are playing an instrument, speaking, or just making a noise, the way the sound is made, and the way it travels, is exactly the same.

The difference between music and noise is that musical sounds are organized into patterns with pitch and rhythm, while noise is usually made up of random, disorganized sounds.

HOW SOUND TRAVELS

A sound is made when something vibrates and makes particles in the air next to it vibrate. The air particles pass the vibration from one to another. You can describe a sound by showing it on a graph. The shape is called a sound wave. Different sounds have different shaped sound waves. The number of times a sound wave vibrates each second is called frequency. A high note has a high frequency.

Above is what a sound wave looks like on a graph.

Trumpet

SOUND WAVES

The look of a sound wave varies according to what is making the sound. These sound waves are all produced by different instruments.

Internet link

For a link to a website about sound waves, go to **www.usborne-quicklinks.com**

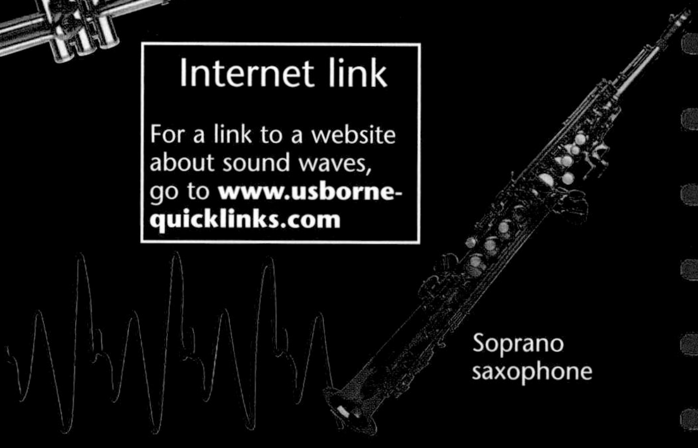

Soprano saxophone

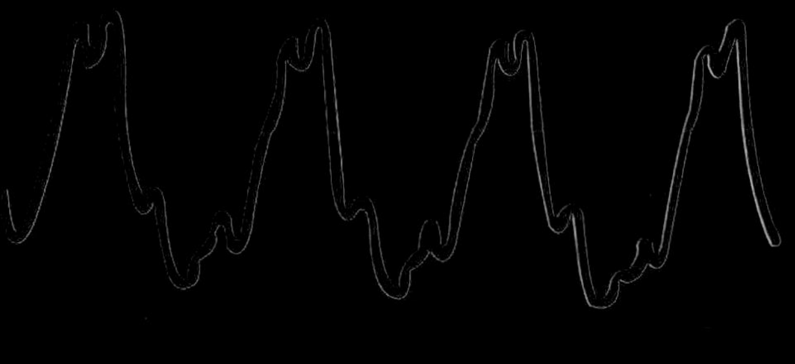

Violin

ELECTRONIC INSTRUMENTS

A lot of bands use electronic instruments, such as drum machines and keyboards. These sorts of instruments use a computer chip to store and reproduce sound waves.

STORING SOUND

A chip doesn't store the sound itself; it stores numbers which describe a sound wave. The numbers indicate the height of the wave measured at regular intervals.

DRUM MACHINES

Drum machines are electronic devices that store pre-set sounds made by percussion instruments, such as cymbals, drums or maracas. You choose a sound and then play a rhythm by tapping on pads (see below).

PLAYING WITH SOUNDS

A keyboard is designed to store the sound waves produced by musical instruments, but it can also reproduce other sounds, such as a bird tweeting. This is done using a machine called a sampler. Some keyboards have sampled sounds. Once the sound has been stored, you can play tunes with it. You can even alter the sound by reversing it, or making it echo.

You can have great fun experimenting with sounds which have been stored on a keyboard. Imagine playing Mozart with a bird tweeting for each note!

You can choose sounds and play rhythms by tapping on these pads.

You can also record a rhythm and play it back, so you can play another instrument alongside the rhythm. Rhythms can also be made faster or slower. Most drum machines have pre-set rhythms. These can be useful if you don't want to make up your own.

Music to listen to

VIOLIN MUSIC
J.S. Bach, Partita no. 1 in b minor, BWV 1002
Martin Hayes and Dennis Cahill, *The Lonesome Touch* (1977)

TRUMPET MUSIC
Miles Davis, *Kind of Blue* (1959)

SAXOPHONE MUSIC
World saxophone quartet, *Dances and Ballads* (1987)

ELECTRONIC MUSIC
Groove Armada, *Vertigo* (1999)

THE COMPOSER

Anyone who makes up music is a composer, although the title is most often used to describe people who write classical music. A composer's imagination can be triggered by anything: a person, an event, nature, or even a musical theme. Most composers don't rely on inspiration alone, though. They also need technical skills to help put their musical ideas down on paper.

The top manuscript on the left is one of Mozart's. The one below was written by Beethoven.

HOW COMPOSERS WORK

Some composers can write down music as soon as it comes into their heads. Others spend a long time developing their ideas first. Composers often jot down melodies or rhythms when they think of them and use them later for new compositions. The structure of a piece is usually planned early on, though, so the composer can work within a framework.

You can tell a lot about how famous composers worked by looking at their manuscripts and sketchbooks. Beethoven probably made more pages of musical jottings than any other composer of his time. Some of the sketches are only fragments of tunes and rhythms, many of which he never used. Others are detailed workings of whole pieces or movements. Beethoven used these sketches mainly as reminders.

Mozart, on the other hand, usually worked out compositions in his head first, down to the last detail, before writing anything down.

Blues musician W.C. Handy composing at the piano

In Renaissance and Baroque times, European courts employed composers and musicians. This picture, from the 1700s, shows court musicians entertaining noblemen.

PATRONAGE

Before around 1750, most composers were employed either by the Church or by the courts of nobles. This system is known as patronage. In Europe, most cathedrals had their own choir and orchestra. Composers had to provide music for Sundays and religious festivals. Court composers also had to compose for a variety of events. From around 1750, the system of patronage started to decline. Composers began to make a living by having their music played at public concerts, as well as teaching or performing.

Their lives became more independent, as they began to be paid, or commissioned, to write new music for a range of different wealthy people and organizations. Many composers also had their music published, which helped to spread their reputations.

Internet links

For links to websites where you can explore the lives of different composers, go to
www.usborne-quicklinks.com

Music to listen to

Handel: *Music for the Royal Fireworks* (written in 1749 to celebrate the end of war in Europe)

Benjamin Britten: *War Requiem* (written in 1961 for the opening of Coventry cathedral, in the UK)

W.C. Handy, *W.C. Handy's Memphis Blues Band* (1917/1994)

THE PERFORMER

When a composer writes a piece of music, there is a limit to the instructions that he or she can put down on paper. It is up to the performer to interpret the music and bring it to life. This is why the same piece can sound very different, depending on who is playing. The better the performer, the better the music will sound. In traditional music and jazz, the performers often play a part in composing as well, improvising as they play.

PLAYING TO AN AUDIENCE

Playing in public can be nerve-wracking. Once the performer has started playing though, concentrating on the music usually replaces the fear. On the right, there are hints to help new performers.

INTERPRETING MUSIC

When a composer writes a piece of music, the written music provides the performer with a guide as to how the music should be played: which notes to play, whether they should be loud or soft, and roughly what speed the piece should be played. Part of the skill of being a good performer, though, is in making decisions about all these things. This is called interpretation.

Because no two performers make exactly the same decisions, no two performances of the same piece ever sound exactly the same. For example, there might be slight differences in speed, or some parts might sound louder or softer. The person in charge of interpreting music for a large group of players is usually the conductor. You can find out more about a conductor's job on the opposite page.

- Appear confident on the stage. Don't shuffle on.

- Play with conviction: the audience is more likely to relax and enjoy themselves.

- Know the piece well: the better you know it, the more confident you are likely to be.

- If you make a mistake, don't go back and correct it. Just keep going and forget all about it. Chances are, no one will have noticed anyway.

- If there is a conductor, try to keep him or her in view as much as possible. Try not to bury your head in the music.

- If you are part of a group, listen to the other musicians so that you can adjust your playing to fit in with them.

THE CONDUCTOR

The conductor is in charge of directing a group of musicians, such as an orchestra or choir. This is done using a range of hand gestures, head and body movements, and facial expressions. Most conductors use a type of stick, called a baton, to indicate the number of beats in a measure and the speed of the music. They also use their hands to tell the players how the music should be played, for example, loudly or quietly, and when they should start playing. This is called giving a cue.

The conductor gives a cue by looking directly, or pointing, at an instrument or section of the orchestra or choir.

This conductor's small hand movements tell the players to play quietly. Large hand movements tell them to play loudly.

HOW CONDUCTING DEVELOPED

The smaller the group of instruments, the less the need for a conductor to keep them together. In the 1700s, when orchestras were small, the harpsichord player or chief violinist would direct the music from their place in the orchestra. In the 1800s, as orchestras got bigger, the custom of conducting with a baton was introduced.

THE CONDUCTOR'S JOß

The conductor studies the music, then decides how it should be played. He or she has to make sure that the musicians are in time with each other, and that none of the instruments is out of tune.

Conductor and composer Leonard Bernstein has a particularly flamboyant conducting style.

Internet links

For links to websites about conducting and famous conductors, go to **www.usborne-quicklinks.com**

Music to listen to

You could compare two different recordings of the same piece. For example, try listening to Mozart's *Eine Kleine Nachtmusik* recorded by the Berlin Philharmonic Orchestra, and by the Orpheus Chamber Orchestra.

BALLET

Ballet tells a story using music and dance, often with amazing costumes and scenery. There are no spoken words, so the dancers tell the story with their movements alone. The music provides a framework for the ballet and helps to build the mood and atmosphere of the story. The people who come up with the sequence of dance steps for ballets are called choreographers.

This is the Sugar Plum Fairy from *The Nutcracker* by Tchaikovsky. Ballet costumes have to make the character's identity especially obvious, because there is no speech.

HOW BALLET BEGAN

In the 16th and 17th centuries, European kings and queens, especially in France and Italy, employed dancing masters to teach their courtiers to move and behave, and to give dancing lessons. Courtiers regularly took part in court entertainments, combining poetry, music and dance. The dances they performed developed into the first ballets.

16th and 17th century dancers wore heavy costumes that limited their movements.

DANCING IN OPERAS

King Louis XIV of France, who ruled from 1643-1715, was a keen dancer. His court composer, Jean-Baptiste Lully, developed works called *opéra-ballets*. These included sections of opera and ballet, in which the King himself often danced. In the ballet sections, the story was spoken or sung by a narrator.

BALLET COMES INTO ITS OWN

By about 1750, ballet had broken away from opera. Jean-Georges Noverre, a leading choreographer, worked with Rameau and other composers to produce ballet with a dramatic plot and no narration, in which the dancers used mime to tell the story. Noverre's ideas changed ballet forever.

Internet links

For links to websites where you can listen to ballet music and watch video clips of performances, go to **www.usborne-quicklinks.com**

CLASSICAL BALLET

The term Classical ballet is used to mean a type of ballet first produced in Russia around the end of the 19th century. Classical ballets usually include lots of complicated and elaborate dance steps to show off the dancers' skills. The Russian composer Tchaikovsky provided music for many famous ballets of the time, including *Swan Lake* and *The Nutcracker*.

These dancers are wearing typical Classical ballet costumes.

Music to listen to

EARLY BALLET
Lully, *Le Bourgeois Gentilhomme*
Rameau, *Castor et Pollux*

CLASSICAL BALLET
Tchaikovsky, *Swan Lake*

MODERN BALLET
Stravinsky, *Firebird*
Prokofiev, *Cinderella*

THE BALLETS RUSSES

Around the end of the 19th century, some people believed that ballet had become mere gymnastics. Choreographers seemed to design ballets just to display the dancers' abilities, and their steps added little to the atmosphere or story. Then, at the start of the 20th century, the Russian director Sergei Diaghilev set up a company called the Ballets Russes. Diaghilev's new company revitalized ballet by giving dance, music and design equal importance. He commissioned new work from composers such as Maurice Ravel (*Daphnis and Chloë*) and Igor Stravinsky (*Firebird, Petrushka* and *The Rite of Spring*).

BALLET TODAY

Composers and choreographers of ballets today have many past styles to draw upon. They also borrow from other kinds of music and dance, such as jazz and folk. Composers of ballets sometimes use different types of modern music, including electronic and aleatory music.

Vaslav Nijinsky (1889-1950) was one of the most famous Ballets Russes dancers and choreographers.

51

SINGING

People have different ideas about what makes a good voice. What sounds perfectly normal to you, might sound very strange to someone from another part of the world. Chinese opera singers, for instance, produce a twangy, nasal tone, while Western opera singers make a fuller sound.

Internet links

For links to websites where you can listen to throat singing and find tips and videos on how to improve your own singing, go to **www.usborne-quicklinks.com**

THROAT SINGING

In certain parts of Central Asia, especially the Russian republic of Tuva, and Mongolia, there is an extraordinary style of singing known as throat singing. By manipulating the mouth, tongue and a cavity at the back of the mouth called the pharynx, throat singers can sing two notes at the same time. Some can even sing up to four notes. The sound they make is like the sound of a flute.

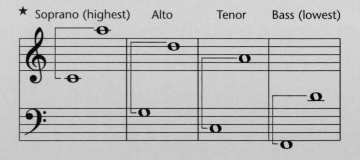

A Tuvan throat singer

HOW YOUR VOICE WORKS

Your voice works by making air particles vibrate, in the same way that a musical instrument does. At the top of your windpipe, is your voicebox, or larynx, and stretched across it are two pieces of skin called the vocal cords. When you breathe, the cords loosen to let the air past, but when you sing or speak, muscles pull the cords tight. The pressure of air squeezing out between them causes them, and the air around them, to vibrate. This is what makes the sound. The air also vibrates in your throat, mouth, chest and nasal cavities, which amplifies the sound. Your breath carries the sound out of your mouth.

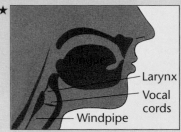

Here you can see the parts of your body used for singing.

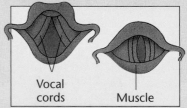

Vocal cords are loose for breathing. The tighter the cords the higher the sound.

VOCAL RANGE

Everyone finds it a strain to sing above and below certain pitches. This is because each voice has its own limits, or vocal range. Everyone's vocal cords, throat, chest and nasal cavaties vary in size and shape. All this affects the shape of the sound waves produced, which makes every voice unique. Most voices, however, fall roughly into one of the types below. Each pair of notes shows the vocal range of each kind of voice.

★ Soprano (highest)   Alto   Tenor   Bass (lowest)

SINGING WITH OTHERS

Singing in a choir where groups of people sing different notes is called part-singing. The different voices in a choir are usually grouped according to their vocal range: sopranos, altos, tenors and basses.

Sometimes, some or all of the parts in a choir are split into two separate sections, called firsts and seconds. For instance, there might be first and second soprano parts, or first and second alto parts.

IMPROVE YOUR SINGING

It's usually easier to sing a note accurately if you imagine it before you sing it. Hearing the note in your head helps your brain to send a message to your throat muscles.

Before you sing, try to relax, so that air can flow uninterrupted from your lungs, out through your throat. Tension can make your throat muscles tighten up, producing a strangled sound.

Breathe in deeply before you sing. You need breath both to make a sound and to carry it out of your body. Try to breathe out steadily. If you don't, the notes may wobble or waver out of tune as the air pressure in your larynx alters.

Singer Robbie Williams is well known for his energetic performances.

★

Soloists   Conductor   Soloists

Here you can see a plan of how the different parts of a choir might be arranged. When an orchestra plays with a choir, it is usually placed in front of the choir.

Music to listen to

SOPRANO
Jessye Norman, *Jessye Norman: Classics* (1992)

ALTO
Olga Borodina (alto) and Dmitri Hvorostovsky, *Arias and Duets* (1998)

TENOR
José Carreras, *Cançiones* (2000)

BASS
Willard White and others, *Gershwin - Porgy and Bess Highlights*

THE STORY OF OPERA I

Opera combines music and drama, elaborate costumes and scenery to create a spectacular form of entertainment. As well as reflecting new musical trends, opera composers have sometimes used it as a way of commenting on social and political events of the day.

Internet link

For a link to a fascinating virtual opera house, where you'll find lots of opera stories, information about composers, sound clips and more, go to **www.usborne-quicklinks.com**

Opera singers often wear masks as part of their costumes.

HOW OPERA BEGAN

In the late 1500s, a group of Italian poets and composers, known as the *Camerata*, began to experiment with new ways of writing songs. They felt that songs were too complicated, so they tried to make their music simple and memorable. They began to apply their ideas to musical plays. Gradually these became known as operas.

This is a scene from an opera called *Lisimaco*, written in 1681 by an Italian composer called Giovanni Maria Pagliardi.

EARLY PERFORMANCES

The first operas were performed in the homes of wealthy noblemen but, as they became more popular, special opera houses were built for public performances. The first public opera house, Teatro San Cassiano, was opened in Venice in 1637. Soon, opera began to spread throughout Europe.

Like most 17th-century operas, Lisimaco is based on ancient mythology.

17th-century operas often contained special effects, such as clouds moving in the sky, or ships sailing across the ocean. These effects must have appeared very spectacular at that time. In this scene, one of the characters is being lowered on to the stage on a moving cloud.

Music to listen to

EARLY OPERA
Peri, *Euridice*
Monteverdi, *Orfeo*
Lully, *Armide*
Purcell, *Dido and Aeneas*

OPERA SERIA
Handel, *Rinaldo*; *Alcina*
Johann Adolph Hasse, *Didone Abbandonata*

COMIC OPERA
John Gay and Johann Christoph Pepusch, *The Beggar's Opera*
Mozart, *Die Zauberflöte* (The Magic Flute); *Le Nozze di Figaro* (The Marriage of Figaro)

AT THE OPERA

During the 1700s, opera became more popular than ever. This was partly because, as more opera houses were built, people began to use them as social meeting places. While the opera was being performed on stage, the audience played cards and chatted with their friends, only occasionally stopping to watch a well-known scene or song, or a famous singer.

OVERTURES

An overture is a piece of music played by the orchestra before the opera begins. Overtures originated in the brass fanfares used by early opera composers to announce the start of a performance. Today, opera overtures are also played at orchestral concerts. There are also some overtures, called concert overtures, which have been specially written for concerts.

The orchestras used in early operas usually contained whatever instruments were available to composers at the time.

18TH-CENTURY STYLES

Most early 18th-century operas were based on stories from ancient history and mythology. They always had a happy ending, in which the villian was caught and the hero was rewarded for his bravery. In Italy, this type of opera was known as *opera seria*, which means 'serious opera'. Handel wrote lots of operas in this style.

An opera seria was usually divided into a few sections called acts. To lighten the mood, comic scenes called *intermezzi* were often performed between each act. Gradually these comic scenes became so popular that composers began to write whole operas in the style of intermezzi. In Italy, this new comic opera style became known as *opera buffa*. Similar types of comic operas were also developing in other countries. In France, comic opera was known as *opéra comique*, in Germany, as *Singspiel*.

Judith Howard performing in Handel's opera seria *Alcina*, written in 1735

The 19th century was the age of some of the most famous and popular composers of opera. Works by Verdi, Puccini and Wagner are among today's best-known operas. This was the great era of Romanticism, in opera as much as in other forms of music, when composers felt that music should reflect feelings and emotions.

A character from the opera *Falstaff* by Wagner

GRAND OPERA

Grand opera began to develop in France around 1830. It was 'grand' because it involved lavish scenery, and often huge, stirring crowd scenes. The stories were usually heroic tales, often based on legends. Two famous grand opera composers are the German Meyerbeer and the Italian Rossini.

OPERETTA

During the 17th and 18th centuries, the word *operetta* was used to describe a short opera. By the mid-1800s, it had become the name for a new style which had developed from French 18th-century *opéra comique*. These new operettas were light-hearted, with some spoken words as well as songs and dances.

Some of the most famous 19th-century operettas include *Die Fledermaus* (The Bat) by the Austrian Johann Strauss, and *Die Lustige Witwe* (The Merry Widow) by the Hungarian Franz Lehár.

Internet link

For a link to a website where you can take an interactive look at the history of opera, go to **www.usborne-quicklinks.com**

A scene from *Die Fledermaus* by Johann Strauss

EASTERN EUROPE

Opera first spread to Eastern Europe in the early 1700s, but it wasn't until the 19th century that it really began to flourish. Around 1850, 'The Russian Five' began to use opera, as well as other musical forms, to express their Russian identity.

Two of the most famous operas by members of this group were *Boris Godunov*, by Musorgsky, and *Prince Igor* by Borodin, both telling tales from Russian history. *Prince Igor* is about a 12th-century Russian nobleman, who defended his country from Mongol invaders. Borodin uses elements of Russian folk tunes and harmonies in the music.

The character Boris from a performance of the opera *Boris Gudunov* by Musorgsky

A scene from *Prince Igor* by Borodin

20TH-CENTURY OPERA

In the early 1900s, some composers, such as Igor Stravinsky, began to write operas in a neo-Classical style, using the forms and techniques of Baroque and Classical composers. One example of this is Stravinsky's *Mavra*, written in 1922. Other composers have experimented with new ways of writing and performing. For example, the Italian composer Luigi Nono used recorded sounds in his 1961 opera, *Intolleranza 1960*.

A character from a modern opera by Stockhausen, written in 1980

MUSIC FOR FILM AND TELEVISION

Music plays an important part in film and TV, because it provides an excellent way to create atmosphere. It emphasizes the mood of a scene, to show whether it's happy or sad, funny or scary.

Internet links

For links to websites where you can play games to find out how music emphasizes different themes and emotions, go to **www.usborne-quicklinks.com**

THEME MUSIC

In a film, theme music usually sums up the general mood: dramatic, romantic, or action-packed. For TV, it depends on what type of show it is. A soap opera, for example, often has very simple theme music so people can easily recognise it. This also reminds you that the show is on, and calls you to watch.

The theme music for *Star Wars* became very famous. This character is C-3PO from the film.

INCIDENTAL MUSIC

The music you hear during a film or television show is called incidental music. Often this contains variations on the theme tune. Sometimes incidental music is used to let the audience know something is about to happen, or to make them think something is about to happen. Next time you watch a horror movie or a thriller notice how a build up of dramatic music adds to the suspense.

This is the ferocious Velociraptor dinosaur from *Jurassic Park*. Loud, booming drums play when it appears in the film, adding to the terror.

FILM MUSIC

It is the job of the film director to choose a composer to write the music. The director decides which scenes will have music and what sort of music would suit each scene. The composer then needs to time the music so that it fits the action on the screen.

A film is made up of lots of individual pictures, called frames, and there are 24 frames every second. The composer is given the film on video. There is a number on each frame showing hours, minutes, seconds and frames. This tells the composer how far into the film that frame appears, so he or she can determine how long a scene is, and time the music to fit.

John Williams has written the music for many blockbusters, including *Jurassic Park* and *The Star Wars Trilogy*.

This picture of a cinema in the 1920s shows a pianist (on the right) providing the music accompaniment for a silent movie.

MUSIC FOR SILENT MOVIES

Until the 1930s, films did not have soundtracks. Instead, a pianist was usually employed to play or improvise an accompaniment to the film. Common musical themes were developed to accompany different situations, such as love scenes, chase sequences, or scenes in which something frightening was about to take place.

SOUND SYSTEMS

There are usually four sets of speakers in a cinema. Parts of a soundtrack, the music that accompanies a film, come from all sets of speakers. Other parts come from only one or two. This adds to the atmosphere of a film, because the sound is coming from different directions. This system of reproducing sound is called Dolby Stereo.

Here you can see a plan of how speakers are usually positioned in a cinema.

SOUND REPRODUCTION

Sounds are made up of a series of regular vibrations. The way these vibrations are recorded is called sound reproduction.

HOW SOUND IS RECORDED

Until the 1970s, sound was recorded by a process known as analogue recording, whereby sound waves were stored as a continuously varying magnetic pattern. Vinyl records were produced in this way.

★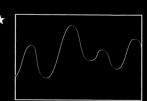

This is what an analogue wave looks like.

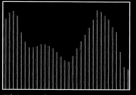

This is the pattern created during a digital recording.

This picture shows a singer being recorded in a recording studio.

In the early 1980s, a far more accurate method, known as digital recording, came into use. This method converts analogue waves into a long series of numbers, and records the numbers. To play the music back, the numbers are converted back into analogue waves. This is how CDs and Mini Discs are recorded. They are much clearer than records.

Internet links

For links to websites where you can take a tour of a recording studio, try out a virtual mixing desk and find an animated explanation of how CDs work, go to **www.usborne-quicklinks.com**

HOW CDs WORK

A CD stores music in digital form. The disc is made of a light, flexible metal, coated with a transparent, protective plastic layer. The metal surface contains millions of tiny pits.

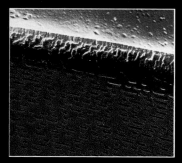

This is what a CD looks like under a microscope. The pits are shown by the red and yellow areas on the green surface. The plastic coating is shown by the blue area on top.

Inside a CD player, a laser beam scans the disc's surface and senses where the pits are. This information is then converted into a series of numbers. These numbers are the measurements of the sound waves which make up the music.

There is no contact between the laser beam and the disc, so they don't wear each other out. The beam is focused on the surface, so it travels through scratches on the plastic coating. This means that CDs tend to be tougher and last longer than vinyl records.

RECORDING

In a recording studio, a piece of music is built up gradually, layer by layer, or instrument by instrument. Each layer is called a track. The tracks are recorded one at a time. This way, if there is a mistake in one part of the recording, say, the piano part, it can be recorded again without having to re-record the whole piece. This is known as multitrack recording.

The producer and sound engineer listen to each track and adjust its tone, volume or speed. When all the tracks have been recorded, they are mixed together at a mixing desk. The final mix is put on a master tape, called a DAT (digital audio tape). CDs, tapes or Mini Discs are then copied from this DAT.

Performers, engineers and producers all get involved in putting together the final mix. Here you can see them seated at the mixing desk.

RECORDING AN ORCHESTRA

★

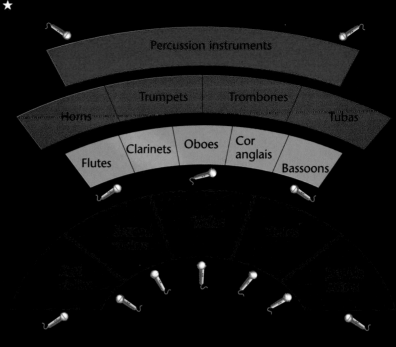

Percussion instruments

Trumpets   Trombones

Horns   Tubas

Clarinets   Oboes   Cor anglais

Flutes   Bassoons

This is how the microphones might be set up for a multitrack recording of an orchestra in a concert hall.

To record a large group, such as an orchestra, on one track the microphones have to be positioned carefully. If they are in the wrong places, one instrument might sound louder than another.

HOW INSTRUMENTS WORK

Most instruments are either electric or acoustic (not electric), and they can be grouped into a few main categories, or families. Although the instruments within these categories come in all different shapes and sizes, the way they work is fundamentally the same.

PERCUSSION INSTRUMENTS

Percussion instruments are ones which make a sound when you hit, shake or scrape them. Hitting, shaking or scraping an instrument causes it to vibrate and produce sound waves. In a drum, for example, some of the waves produced spread down into the hollow part of the drum, where they echo around and grow louder. This is called resonance. There are two types of percussion instruments: pitched and unpitched. A pitched instrument produces one or more musical notes. An unpitched one just makes a noise.

Maracas are an unpitched percussion instrument.

These steel drums are pitched percussion instruments. Different notes are produced, according to where you strike the drums.

STRINGED INSTRUMENTS

Violin strings are stretched over a piece of wood called a bridge. This carries vibrations from the strings to the soundbox.

On a stringed instrument, sound is produced when a string vibrates, by plucking or bowing it. On a violin, a vibrating string makes the air inside the body, or soundbox, vibrate. This makes the whole instrument vibrate and resonate the sound.

Bridge

Soundbox

Music to listen to

PERCUSSION
Evelyn Glennie,
Drumming (1996)

STRINGS
Kronos quartet,
Caravan (2000)
Vivaldi, *The Four Seasons*

WOODWIND
Mozart, Flute quartets
Stravinsky, Symphonies for Wind Instruments

BRASS
Haydn, Trumpet concerto in E flat major

ELECTRONIC INSTRUMENTS
Kraftwerk, *Trans-Europe Express* (1977)

KEYBOARDS
Scott Joplin, *Maple Leaf Rag*
Olivier Messiaen, *Le Banquet Céleste*

Internet link

For a link to a website all about instruments, go to **www.usborne-quicklinks.com**

WIND INSTRUMENTS

There are two types of wind instruments: woodwind and brass. The names come from the materials the original instruments were made of, though many are now made from other materials.

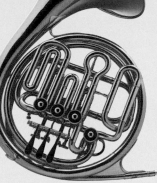

The French horn is a brass instrument.

Wind instruments work by making a column of air inside the instrument vibrate. In woodwind instruments, this is done by blowing over a hole to make the air vibrate, or by blowing onto a strip of cane, or metal, called a reed. In brass instruments, the sound is made by buzzing your lips into a special mouthpiece.

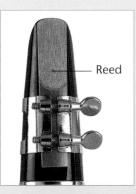

— Reed

Covering holes in the tube makes the air column longer and the note lower. On some instruments, keys cover holes which are too big for a finger to cover. There are levers to operate keys over holes in awkward places.

This is the mouthpiece of a clarinet. A clarinet is a woodwind instrument which has a reed.

ELECTRIC AND ELECTRONIC INSTRUMENTS

An electric instrument uses electricity to amplify the sound waves, instead of a soundbox, or column. An electronic instrument such as a synthesizer uses electricity to make sound, as well as to amplify it.

An electric guitar needs to be connected to a loudspeaker, or amplifier.

KEYBOARD INSTRUMENTS

Keyboard instruments are divided up into those that make sounds from vibrating strings, such as a piano, and those that make sounds from a vibrating column of air, such as an organ.

Inside a piano (see right), a hammer hits a string when a key is pressed.

This is a pipe organ. Rows of pipes are connected to the keyboard. When a key is pressed, the bottom of a pipe opens to let air through. This action is what makes the sound.

THE ORCHESTRA

In classical music, the largest unit of musicians for playing is called an orchestra. Originally, the orchestra was just a group of stringed instruments. Later, other instruments came to be added. Today, orchestras have around one hundred players and are made up of four main groups of instruments: strings, woodwind, brass and percussion. Here is a plan of an orchestra, showing the usual position of each group.

The percussion section may include different instruments from those shown, depending on what is needed for the piece.

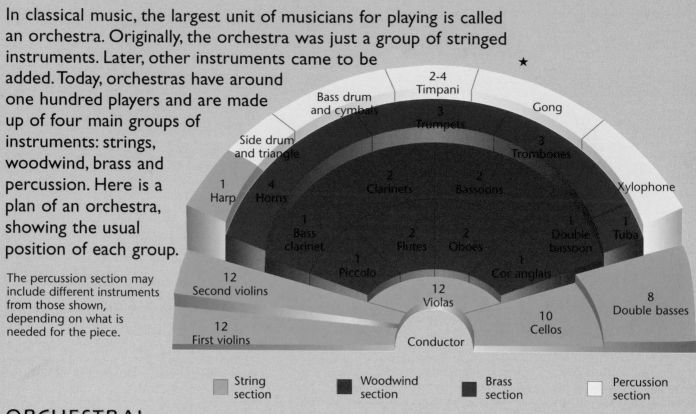

★

2-4 Timpani

Bass drum and cymbals

Gong

3 Trumpets

Side drum and triangle

3 Trombones

1 Harp

4 Horns

2 Clarinets

2 Bassoons

Xylophone

1 Bass clarinet

2 Flutes

2 Oboes

1 Double bassoon

1 Tuba

1 Piccolo

1 Cor anglais

12 Second violins

12 Violas

8 Double basses

10 Cellos

12 First violins

Conductor

■ String section   ■ Woodwind section   ■ Brass section   ☐ Percussion section

ORCHESTRAL MUSIC

Different instruments provide different musical textures and tones. This allows composers scope to create different effects, by choosing certain instruments to play together, balancing and contrasting them. Some orchestral music, such as Romantic symphonies, needs all the instruments shown in the plan above. Many, including works by the composer Gustav Mahler, need even more. Mahler's symphony no.8 in E flat requires so many players that it is known as 'Symphony of a Thousand'. Other music only needs a section of the orchestra. During Baroque times, orchestras were smaller than they are today. Most Baroque orchestral music requires around 30 musicians.

This orchestra is the Rotterdam Philharmonic Orchestra from Rotterdam in the Netherlands. Notice the harps on the right-hand side. The harp is not a standard orchestral instrument, like the violin, and is only included if it is needed for the piece.

A magazine cover from 1946, featuring the Italian conductor Arturo Toscanini (1867-1957)

THE CONDUCTOR

One of the most vital jobs in an orchestra is that of the conductor - the person in charge of making sure that all the musicians play together and keep the same time. A conductor is also responsible for deciding how the music should be played, and for leading rehearsals.

The principal first violinist in an orchestra is called the leader. He or she leads the players in carrying out the conductor's instructions, for example, by suggesting the best way to play some parts.

Yuri Bashmet is a renowned Ukrainian viola player.

Music to listen to

ORCHESTRAL MUSIC
Prokofiev, *Peter and the Wolf*, op. 67
Britten, *The Young Person's Guide to the Orchestra*
Berlioz, *Symphonie Fantastique*

ORCHESTRA WITH SOLOIST
Jacqueline Du Pré, *Les Introuvables de Jacqueline Du Pré* (1999)
Edward Elgar, Cello Concerto

Internet link

For a link to a website where you can explore the orchestra and listen to sound clips, go to **www.usborne-quicklinks.com**

SOLOISTS

There are sections in some orchestral music, usually concertos, for one or more solo instruments. In a concerto, the soloist plays more difficult and complicated music than the orchestra. This makes the soloist's music stand out from the music played by the orchestra.

STRINGED INSTRUMENTS

All instruments belong to one of four families. Over the next six pages you can find out about the main instruments in each family. Stringed instruments produce a sound from the vibration of strings. The main stringed instruments in an orchestra are the violin, viola, cello and double bass.

Internet links

For links to websites where you can listen to sound clips of stringed and woodwind instruments, examine virtual instruments and find interviews with musicians, go to **www.usborne-quicklinks.com**

Orchestral strings
Violin, Viola, Cello, Double Bass

Older stringed instruments
Viols, Viola d'amore, Viola da gamba

Harps and zithers
Koto, Zither, Harp

Guitars and lutes
Acoustic guitar, Lute, Balalaika, Mandolin, Banjo, Sitar, Vina, Tambura, Ukelele

Cello

Viola

Violin

Double bass

Viol

Zither

Koto

Harp

Bouzouki (Greek lute)

Balalaika (Russian lute)

Mandolin

Sitar

Vina

Guitar

Ukelele

Banjo

Lute

WOODWIND INSTRUMENTS

Woodwind instruments make a sound when the player blows into the instrument, causing a column of air inside to vibrate. Piccolos, flutes, oboes, clarinets and bassoons are the ones used in an orchestra. The piccolo is the highest-sounding and the bassoon is the lowest-sounding.

Edge-blown instruments
Recorders: Sopranino, Descant, Treble, Tenor, Bass
Flutes: Piccolo, Concert flute, Alto flute, Bass flute
Other edge-blown instruments
Didjeridoo, Panpipes
Single reed instruments
Clarinets: E flat clarinet, B flat clarinet, A clarinet
Bassett horn
Saxophones: Soprano sax, Alto sax, Tenor sax, Baritone sax
Double reed instruments
Oboe, Cor anglais, Bassoon, Double or contrabassoon
Free reed instruments
Bagpipes, Concertina, Accordion, Mouth organ

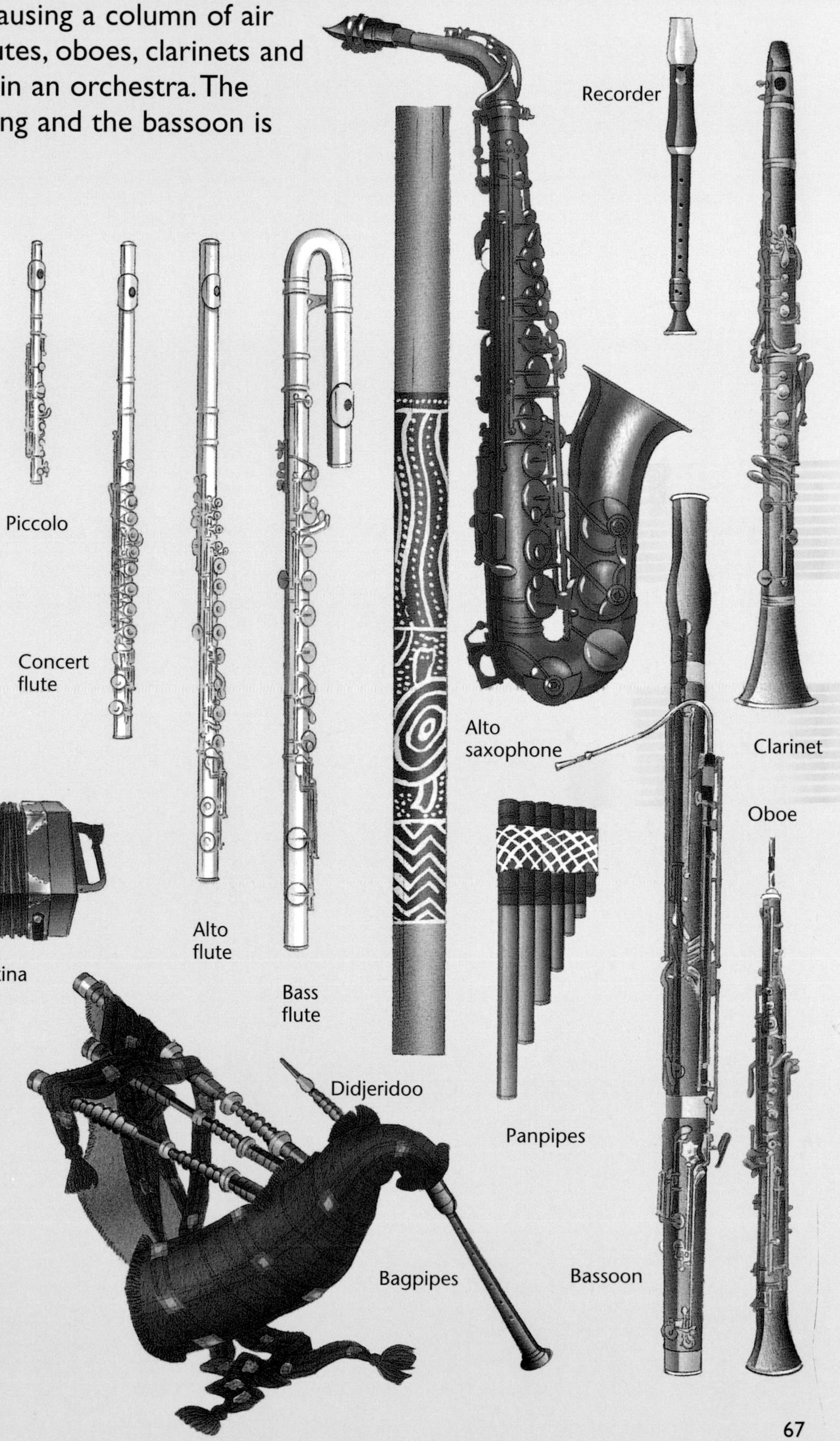

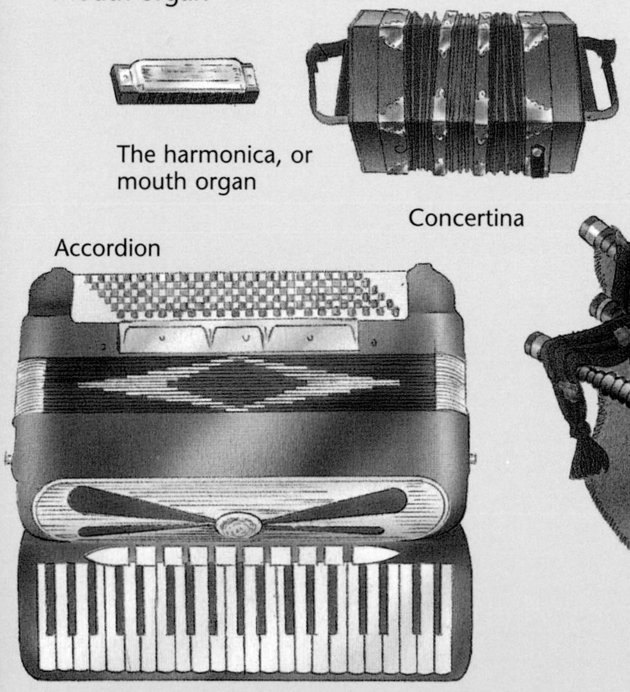

Recorder

Piccolo

Concert flute

The harmonica, or mouth organ

Concertina

Accordion

Alto flute

Bass flute

Alto saxophone

Bagpipes

Didjeridoo

Panpipes

Clarinet

Oboe

Bassoon

BRASS INSTRUMENTS

Brass instruments are metal wind instruments. They were originally made of brass, but nowadays other metals are often used. The sound is made when the player's lips, vibrating against a mouthpiece, causes a column of air inside the instrument to vibrate. Brass instruments used in an orchestra are the trumpet, trombone, French horn and tuba.

Trumpets
Natural trumpet, Standard B flat trumpet, Piccolo trumpet

Trombones
Tenor trombone, Tenor/bass trombone

Horns
French or double horn, Bugle, B flat cornet, B flat flügelhorn

Saxhorns
E flat tenor horn, B flat baritone, B flat tenor tuba or euphonium, E flat bass tuba, Sousaphone

Trumpet

Piccolo trumpet

Tenor trombone

French horn

Cornet

Bugle

E flat tenor horn

B flat bass or euphonium

E flat bass tuba

Sousaphone

Internet links

For links to websites with sound clips and information about brass and percussion instruments, go to **www.usborne-quicklinks.com**

PERCUSSION INSTRUMENTS

Percussion instruments make a sound when you hit, scrape or shake them. They are either tuned (to produce musical notes) or untuned (they just make a noise). The percussion instruments used in an orchestra vary according to the piece being performed.

★

Hi-hat cymbals

Cymbals

Tom-toms

Floor tom

Clash cymbals

Bass drum

Side or snare drum

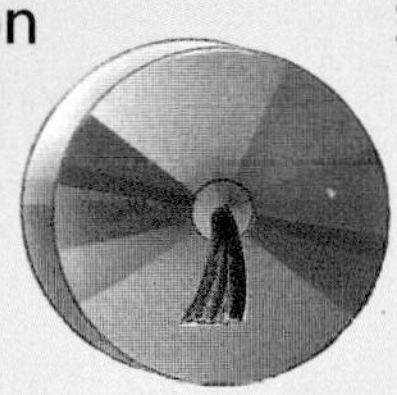

UNTUNED PERCUSSION

Drums
Side or snare drum, Tom-tom, Tenor drum, Bass drum, Bongos, Conga, Timbales

Clappers
Claves, Castanets, Whip, Slapstick

Rattles
Maracas, Cabaca

Slit drums
Wood block, Log drum

Cymbals
Clash cymbals, Crash cymbals, Hi-hat cymbals, Finger cymbals

Other untuned percussion instruments
Gong or tamtam, Tambourine, Triangle, Wind machine, Guiro

Conga drum

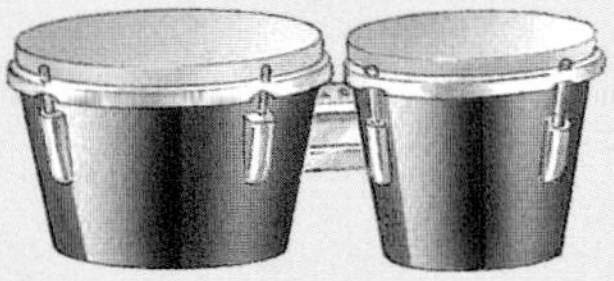

Bongos

Claves

Slapstick

Castanets

Maracas

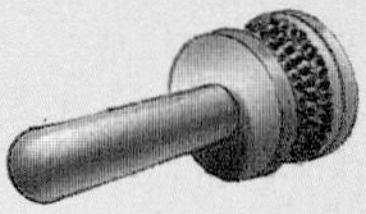

Cabaca

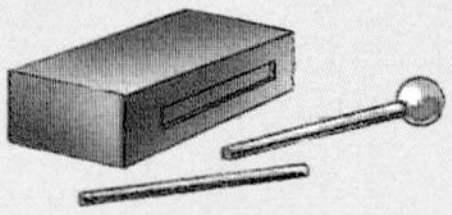

Wood block

TUNED PERCUSSION

Xylophones
Xylophone, Marimba

Metallophones
Vibraphone, Glockenspiel, Celesta

Chimes
Tubular bells, Chime bars, Cowbells

Tuned drums
Timpani or kettle drums, Steel drums

Kettle drum

Triangle

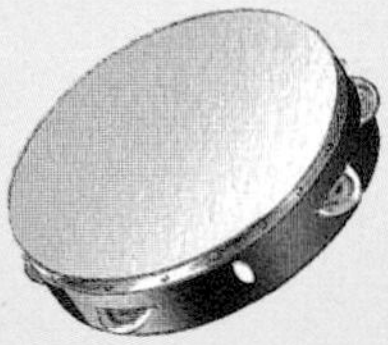

Tambourine

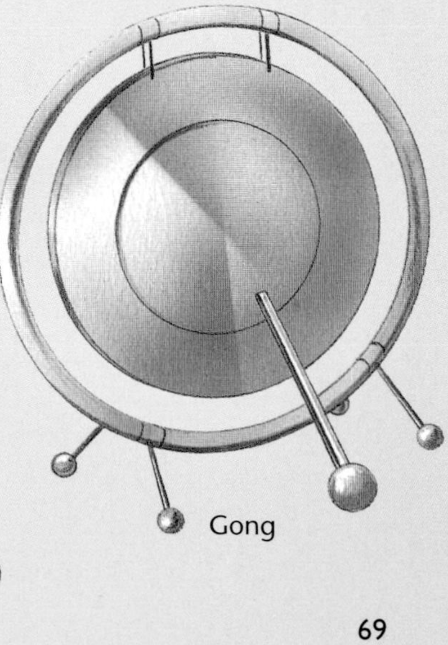

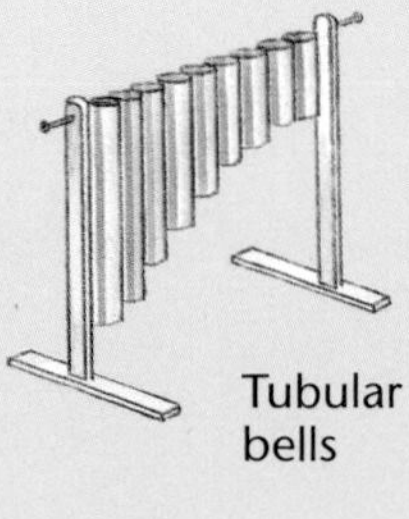

Tubular bells

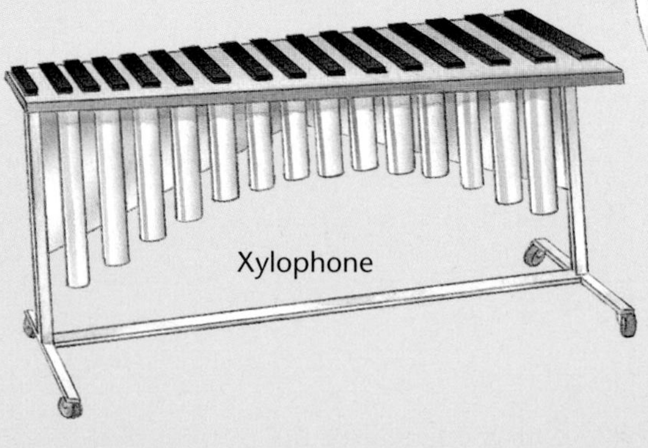

Xylophone

Gong

KEYBOARD INSTRUMENTS

Some keyboard instruments, such as pianos, make a sound from vibrating strings. Others, such as organs, make a sound from vibrating columns of air. Keyboard instruments used to be part of an orchestra, in the 17th and 18th centuries, but nowadays they are mostly used as solo instruments.

★

Internet links

For links to websites all about pianos and other keyboard instruments, go to **www.usborne-quicklinks.com**

Stringed keyboard instruments
Clavichord, Harpsichord, Spinet, Upright piano, Grand piano
Wind keyboard instruments
Pipe organ, Harmonium

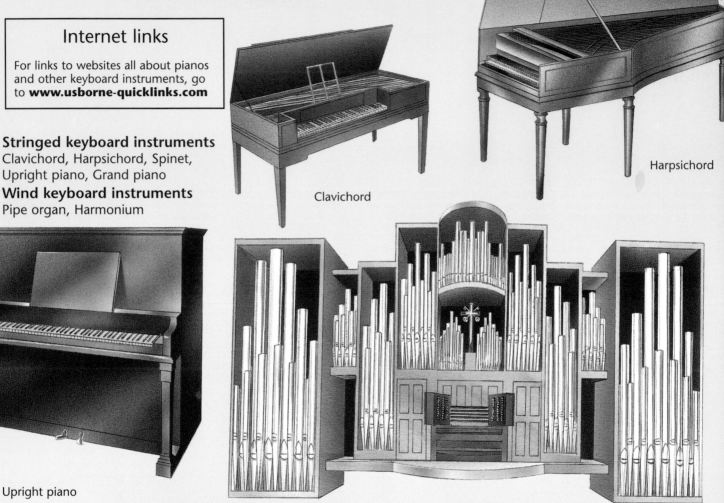

Clavichord

Harpsichord

Upright piano

Pipe organ

Grand piano

Harmonium

ELECTRIC & ELECTRONIC INSTRUMENTS

In electric instruments, the sound is amplified electronically rather than by the body of the instrument. Electronic instruments use electricity to create the sounds themselves as well as to amplify them.

Electric instruments
Electric guitar, Bass guitar, Electric organ, Electric violin

Electronic instruments
Synthesizer, Drum machine, Theramin, Ondes Martenot

Electric violin

★

Electric guitar

Synthesizer

Drum machine

The ondes martenot is an electronic keyboard instrument that was invented in 1928. It makes a weird, haunting sound.

Bass guitar

LEARNING AN INSTRUMENT

Learning an instrument can be very rewarding, and lots of fun, but you have to work hard to play well. If you want to learn an instrument, it's important to choose one carefully. You need to think about which ones you like the sound of and what type of music you want to play.

Internet link

For a link to a website with information on different brands of instruments, as well as tips for taking care of your instrument, go to **www.usborne-quicklinks.com**

FINDING A TEACHER

For recommendations, you could ask the music staff at your school or college. If possible, talk to a teacher's existing pupils to get an idea of what he or she is like, and what kind of training is provided. Alternatively, your local library probably has a list of teachers in your area. A music shop may also know of local teachers or carry their advertisements, or you could look in a local newspaper or search the Internet.

GETTING AN INSTRUMENT

You might be able to borrow a school instrument, especially if your school band or orchestra needs players. Brass bands usually lend instruments to their members on long-term loan.

New instruments can be expensive to buy, but you can hire them. This is a good option if you're not sure which instrument you would like to learn. Most music shops hire instruments out fairly cheaply.

BUYING NEW

Generally, the more you pay, the better the instrument. Most instruments, except electric instruments, hold their value well for future sale second-hand. To help with the cost of buying a new instrument, lots of shops operate a hire-purchase scheme. There is a rough guide to the relative cost of new instruments on the opposite page.

The choice of instruments in a shop can be bewildering. It's a good idea to find out about different brands before you buy.

BUYING SECOND-HAND

Before you buy an instrument, either new or second-hand, it's a good idea to have it checked by someone else. For example, if you know an experienced player, or a teacher, bring him or her along with you.

Second-hand stores should let you try out an instrument before you buy it. Be suspicious if they are unwilling to provide at least a year's guarantee. You may see advertisements for instruments in newspapers, or on the Internet, but be careful, as these instruments don't usually have a guarantee.

Instrument	Cost	Ease of playing / potential
FLUTE	Moderate	The flute is quite easy for beginners unless you are left-handed. Very thick or very thin lips, large front teeth or wearing a brace, can make it difficult to blow.
CLARINET	Moderate	The clarinet is easier to blow than the flute and you can make progress quite quickly. Strong front teeth are a positive advantage.
OBOE	Very expensive	The oboe is a difficult instrument. It helps to have thin lips which you can fold over your teeth to grip the reed.
SAXOPHONE	Expensive	A saxophone is easier than a flute or clarinet. It's a good choice if you're not very interested in classical music.
RECORDER	From very cheap to very expensive, depending on the quality	Basic technique is not too difficult but, like any instrument, advanced technique needs a lot of skill.
TRUMPET	Moderate	A trumpet is quite hard to blow, and it makes a loud, bright sound.
TUBA	Very expensive	The tuba is big but needs less puff than a trumpet. The music isn't usually difficult and you rarely have to play it fast.
FRENCH HORN	Very expensive	This orchestral and solo instrument probably has a greater role in classical music than any other brass instrument.
VIOLIN	Moderate	It's not easy to make nice sounds on a violin. It may be a year or two before you can produce a really good tone.
VIOLA	Moderate	Most viola music is easier than violin music, but the viola is bigger than the violin so your fingers have to move further.
PIANO	Very expensive	While you are learning the piano, there is lots of music to play at every level.
CELLO	Expensive	The cello is easier for beginners than the violin, but the advanced technique requires the same skill.
DOUBLE BASS	Very expensive	Most, but not all, of the orchestral music is fairly simple. The double bass often has solos in jazz bands though, which can be difficult. It helps to have large, strong hands.
CLASSICAL GUITAR	From cheap to expensive, depending on the quality	Classical guitar is not easy to play. Your fingers need to do different things quickly and with great precision.
ELECTRIC AND BASS GUITAR	Moderate	It is not difficult to pick up chord technique, strumming and picking on an electric guitar. A bass is quite easy as you usually play only one note at a time.
DRUMS	A kit is expensive	Learning to play drums well takes several years. You need a good sense of rhythm. Drums are very loud, but you can muffle the sound fairly easily for practicing.

READING MUSIC I

Reading music is important if you sing or play an instrument. It will also help you to understand and enjoy all kinds of music. The next six pages explain how music is written down.

Internet link

For links to websites where you can play games to help you learn how to read music, go to **www.usborne-quicklinks.com**

NOTE LENGTHS

In music, notes usually last for a particular length of time. The length of each note is measured in steady counts called beats. The shape of a note shows how many beats it lasts for. On the right is a reminder of the note lengths explained on page 25.

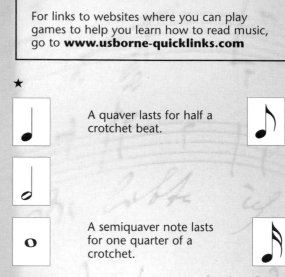

A crotchet lasts for one beat.

A minim lasts for two beats.

A semibreve lasts for four beats.

A quaver lasts for half a crotchet beat.

A semiquaver note lasts for one quarter of a crotchet.

TIME SIGNATURES

Music is divided into sections called bars, with each bar separated from the next one by a line called a bar-line. At the beginning of the staff, a sign called a time signature tells you how many beats there are in each bar.

The numbers at the beginning of a piece of music are the time signature. Some different time signatures are shown on the right. In all time signatures, the top number shows how many beats there are in each bar, and the bottom number shows what kind of beats they are.

Normally, the first beat of a bar sounds slightly stronger than the others. Try clapping the rhythm patterns on the right to hear the rhythms, making the first note of each bar a little louder than the others.

This top number four tells you there are four beats in each bar.

Bar-lines separate the bars.

This bottom number four tells you they are crotchet.

At the end of a piece of music, there is usually a double bar-line.

This number three shows there are three beats in each bar.

This number eight shows they are quaver beats.

This time signature shows there are two minim beats in each bar.

Two crotchets last as long as one minim.

DOTTED NOTES

A dot after a note makes it half as long again. Here you can see how long each kind of dotted note lasts.

A dotted crotchet lasts for one and a half crotchet beats.

★

A dotted quaver lasts for one and a half quaver beats.

A dotted minim lasts for three crotchet beats.

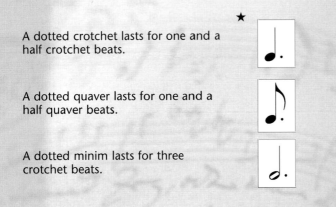

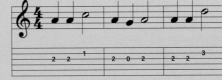

SILENCES IN MUSIC

A silence in music is called a rest. There are symbols that show how long each rest lasts. Here are some of the main ones:

A crotchet rest lasts for one beat's silence.

★

A minim rest lasts for two beats' silence.

A semibreve rest lasts for four beats' silence.

A quaver rest lasts for half a beat's silence.

A semiquaver note rest lasts for a quarter of a beat's silence.

A dotted crotchet rest has a dot after a crotchet rest. All dotted note rests work in a similar way.

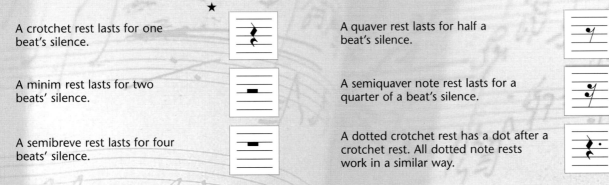

USING RESTS

A bar of music must contain the full number of beats, even if some of those beats are silent. Look at these examples to see how this works.

A crotchet rest lasts for one beat.

The time signature is 4/4, so the notes and rests in each bar add up to four beats.

A full bar's rest is represented by a semibreve rest whatever the time signature. Below, you can see some examples.

Rest for one full bar (two beats)

Here, the time signature is 3/4, so the notes and rests in each bar add up to three beats.

Rest for one full bar (three beats)

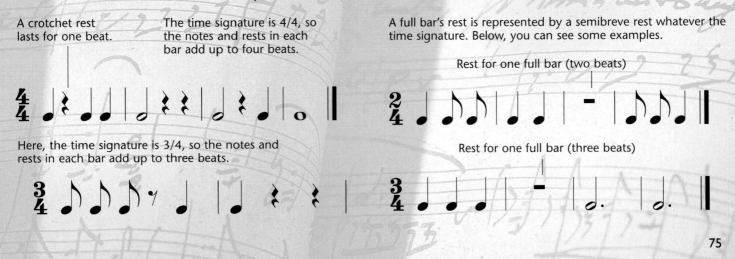

READING MUSIC II

UPBEATS

Sometimes there are notes at the beginning of a piece that don't make up a full bar. These are called upbeats. The beats in the first and last bars add up to a full bar.

One beat at the beginning

Two beats at the end

Two beats at the beginning

Two beats at the end

TIED NOTES

A note can be made longer by joining it to another with a curved line called a tie. When you see a tie, you play the first note and hold it for the length of both notes added together.

A minim tied to a crotchet lasts for three beats.

Tied notes can cross a bar-line. These tied crotchets last for two beats.

TRIPLETS

A composer might want to fit three quavers into the time of one crotchet beat. There is no note symbol which stands for a third of a crotchet. Instead, a number three is written over the notes. The group of quavers shown below is called a triplet.

All three notes should be played in the time of one crotchet beat.

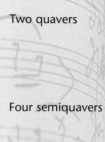

MAKING MUSIC EASIER TO READ

Groups of quavers and shorter notes, such as semiquavers, can be joined together with one or more lines to make them easier to read. These lines are often known as beams. Groups of quavers are usually joined with a single line, while semiquavers are joined with two lines. On the right, you can see some different groupings.

Two quavers

Four semiquavers

One quaver and two semiquavers

Dotted quaver and one semiquaver

Dotted quaver, a semiquaver and a quaver

Two semiquavers and two quavers

GROUPING NOTES AND RESTS

How notes and rests are grouped together depends on the time signature of the music. In some time signatures, called simple time, the groups are based on the type of beat shown by the bottom number in the time signature. But in others, called compound time, they are based on longer beats. Find out more about grouping notes in simple and compound time on this page.

SIMPLE TIME

In simple time, each beat is worth a quaver, crotchet or minim. Notes and rests are grouped together in each bar according to these beats. As a general rule, when the beats can be divided into two equal parts, the music is said to be in simple time.

You can see some examples of groupings in simple time on the right. If you like, you could try writing some rhythms in simple time signatures other than the ones used in the examples.

Here are some simple time signatures:

Bars divided into minim beats	Bars divided into crotchet beats	Bars divided into quaver beats
2/2 3/2 4/2	2/4 3/4 4/4	2/8 3/8 4/8

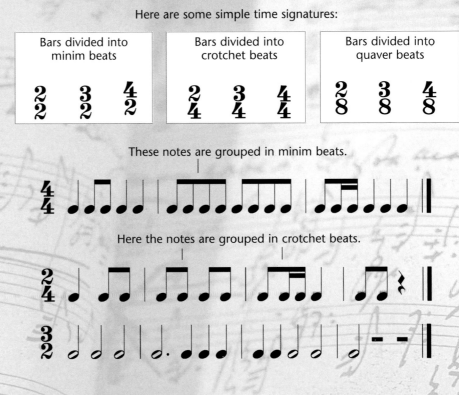

These notes are grouped in minim beats.

Here the notes are grouped in crotchet beats.

COMPOUND TIME

In compound time, bars are divided into beats which last for the length of a dotted note. The beats in compound time can usually be divided into three equal parts. One of the most common compound time signatures is 6/8 time. This signature has two beats in each bar, and each beat is the length of a dotted crotchet. In 6/8 time, notes and rests are grouped in values of a dotted crotchet. On the right, there are some examples of groupings in compound time.

Here are some compound time signatures:

Bars divided into dotted crotchets	Bars divided into dotted minims	Bars divided into dotted quavers
6/8 9/8 12/8	6/4 9/4 12/4	6/16 9/16 12/16

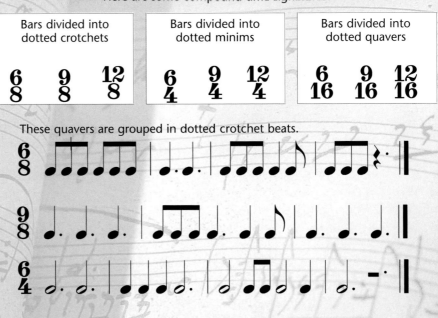

These quavers are grouped in dotted crotchet beats.

READING MUSIC III

NOTE NAMES

Here you can see the positions of notes on the staff, and their corresponding names.

SHARPS AND FLATS

A sharp sign before a note makes that note a semitone higher. To play a sharp note on a keyboard instrument, you press the black key immediately to the right of that note, with no keys in between.

This is a sharp sign.

This note is F sharp.

On a keyboard instrument, play F sharp with the black key immediately to the right of F, with no keys in between.

A flat sign before a note makes that note a semitone lower. On a keyboard instrument, you can play a flat note by pressing the black key immediately to the left of that note, with no keys in between.

This is a flat sign

This note is B flat

Play B flat with the black key immediately to the left of B, with no keys in between.

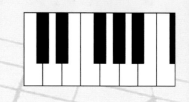

USING SHARPS AND FLATS

A sharp or flat affects any notes on the same line or space after it in the measure. A bar-line cancels a sharp or flat, so the same note in the next measure is not a sharp or flat, unless it has its own sign, or it's in the key signature (see opposite page).

This bar-line cancels the flat.

This note is B flat.

This note is ordinary B again.

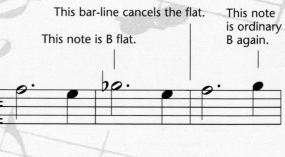

MAJOR SCALES

On the right, you can see the pattern of tones and semitones in the scale of C major. All major scales have the same pattern of tones and semitones, so you can build a major scale on any note, but it must have the same pattern of tones and semitones as the scale of C major. To keep this pattern, other major scales have to use one or more black notes on the keyboard instead of white ones.

Here you can see the pattern of tones and semitones in the scale of C major.

This is the scale of G major. It has one sharp note, F sharp.

The scale of F major has one flat note, B flat.

MINOR SCALES

There are two forms of minor scales: harmonic and melodic. In the melodic minor scale, the pattern of tones and semitones varies according to whether the notes are going up or down. Harmonic minor scales contain an interval of three semitones, or one and a half tones, which isn't very easy to sing.

★ The scale of A harmonic minor

T S T T T T½ S

This is called a natural sign. It cancels a sharp or flat sign.

★ The scale of A melodic minor

T S T T T T S T T S T T S T

RELATIVE SCALES

The last three notes of any major scale form the first three notes of a minor scale. For instance, the last three notes of the scale of C major are the same as the first three notes of A minor. A minor is known as the relative minor scale of C major. C major is A minor's relative major.

C major

A harmonic minor

KEYS AND KEY SIGNATURES

A piece based around the scale of C major is said to be in the key of C major. In some keys, there are sharps or flats next to the clef. They tell you that the music is based on the scale that contains those sharps or flats. These signs are called the key signature, and they tell you to play these notes sharp or flat throughout a piece.

A minor scale has the same key signature as its relative major. The seventh note in a minor scale usually needs a sharp sign written in front of it whenever it occurs in the music.

The scale of D major has two sharps: F sharp and C sharp.

This piece has a key signature of two sharps. This means it is in the key of D major.

Both of these notes are F sharp.   This note is C sharp.

Key signature for G major and E minor

Sharpened seventh note (D sharp)

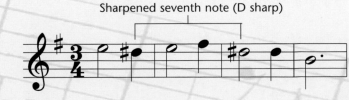

Over the next few pages, you can find out about some famous composers and their music. When a composer's name appears in **bold** type within an entry, there is a separate entry for that composer.

Johann Sebastian BACH (1685-1750)

Bach is considered by many to be the greatest of all classical composers. But during his lifetime, some of his music was very unfashionable. It often sounds dense and complicated - quite unlike the lighter, more tuneful Classical style that was beginning to emerge in the first half of the 18th century. Bach was born into a famous German musical family. He worked at the courts of Weimar and Cöthen before being appointed director of music at St. Thomas's Church, Leipzig, in 1723, where he remained for the rest of his life, composing and performing. He influenced many later composers, including **Mozart**, **Beethoven** and **Mendelssohn**.

Béla BARTÓK (1881-1945)

Born in Hungary, Bartók was taught piano by his mother at an early age. He first composed at the age of eight, first performed in public at 10, and soon became a renowned virtuoso. In the early 1900s, Bartók became interested in Hungarian folk music, and toured the country recording tunes. From around 1908, this music influenced most of his compositions. For example, his works often include rhythms from Hungarian dances, and patterns of notes from folk songs. In 1940, Bartók sadly left war-torn Europe and emigrated to America, where he remained for the rest of his life.

Ludwig van BEETHOVEN (1770-1827)

Beethoven is probably the most influential composer in music history. He developed a new way of writing music that was more complicated than anything written before. Born in Germany, Beethoven went to Vienna, in Austria, where he studied with **Haydn**, and soon became successful as a piano virtuoso. His career as a soloist came to an end, however, when he began to go deaf at the age of 32. Despite this, he continued to compose. In fact, some of his best music was composed after he went totally deaf at the age of 40. But his deafness made him depressed, and he was short-tempered and rude, even to his closest friends. He was enormously popular in Vienna, however, and by the time he died, his fame had spread throughout Europe. He was the first composer to become a public figure, and it is thought that over 10,000 people joined his funeral procession.

Internet link

For a link to a website where you can find out about the lives and works of most major composers, go to
www.usborne-quicklinks.com

Pierre BOULEZ (1925-)

French composer and conductor, Pierre Boulez, studied in Paris with another French composer Olivier Messiaen and later, **Schoenberg**. He took serialism a stage further than Schoenberg had done and applied it, not only to the notes in a piece, but also to other aspects of the music, such as the rhythm and loudness. He has also written aleatory and electronic music, and since the mid-1970s he has concentrated on making music using computers. During the 1950s, Boulez took up conducting, and by the mid-1960s he was conducting lots of famous orchestras, such as the BBC Symphony Orchestra, and the New York Philharmonic Orchestra.

Fryderyk CHOPIN (1810-1849)

Chopin was born near Warsaw in Poland. By the time he was sixteen, he had already begun to make a name for himself as a pianist, playing in small venues in Warsaw, and composing some short piano pieces. He studied at Warsaw Conservatory, and moved to Paris in 1831, where he became famous as a teacher and performer. Chopin gave few large public concerts though, and preferred to play for small groups of people instead. He was never in good health and he died from tuberculosis in 1849. Almost all of his works are for piano, and he often composed while he played. He wrote solo virtuoso pieces, and music for piano and orchestra, as well as simpler music for teaching, and he had a huge influence on later composers including **Wagner**, **Liszt** and **Debussy**.

Claude DEBUSSY (1862-1918)

Debussy, one of the most original composers of the 20th century, was born near Paris, in France. He studied music at the Paris Conservatoire, where he began to experiment with sound and musical ideas. His early works were influenced by Javanese music which he heard in Paris, but he soon became famous as leader of the Impressionistic movement in music. One of his most famous works is *Prélude à 'L'après-midi d'un faune'* for orchestra.

Josquin DEPREZ (Around 1440-1521)

The French-born composer Deprez, or Josquin, as he is often called, is one of the most famous Renaissance composers. He worked at the papal chapel in Rome, and later at the court of Louis XII in France. During his life, Josquin's works influenced many other composers. He wrote mostly religious music, but he also wrote music for entertainment, including around 70 songs.

CLASSICAL COMPOSERS II

Antonin DVORÁK (1841-1904)

Dvorák's music is much influenced by Czech folk music, and he is one of the most famous Czech Nationalist composers. Dvorák's father was a butcher and inn-keeper at the Czech village where he was born. When he was very young, Dvorák used to play simple Czech dances on the fiddle, with his father, for village events. Later, even though his family was very poor, he was given organ and viola lessons. For a time, he played viola in the orchestra of the Czech National Theatre, composing in his spare time. The composer Johannes Brahms (1833-1897) soon discovered his music and, before long, his works were known as far away as England, where he became very popular. In 1892, he accepted a teaching job in New York, but he missed his homeland and family, so he returned to Prague three years later. While he was in New York, he wrote his famous Ninth symphony, better known as 'From the New World'.

George Frideric HANDEL (1685-1759)

Handel is one of the most famous international composers of the Baroque. He was born in Germany, trained in Italy, and lived and worked in England. Unlike other Baroque composers, he didn't rely on wealthy patrons or the church to make a living. Instead, he personally arranged public performances of his music in London, where he lived from around 1712. He wrote mostly Italian operas for these concerts, which were very fashionable at the time. But in the mid-1930s, concert audiences grew tired of opera, so he began to write oratorios instead. Oratorios are like operas but they usually have a religious theme, and there is no scenery, costumes, or acting. Soon, Handel's oratorios became so popular that he never wrote operas again. He was recognized in England, as well as Germany, as the greatest composer of his day.

Joseph HAYDN (1732-1809)

The Austrian composer, Haydn, is perhaps best known for his work in developing the classical symphony and string quartet. He wrote over 100 symphonies and is often called 'the father of the symphony'. He spent most of his life working for the Esterházys, a powerful Hungarian family who lived near Vienna. He had to provide music for two concerts each week, as well as operas and music for church services. Even though he rarely left Vienna, his music was published throughout Europe, and he became very famous during his lifetime.

George GERSHWIN (1898-1937)

Born in New York, in the U.S.A., Gershwin was essentially a self-taught musician. He was a talented songwriter and composed lots of musicals. The lyrics for most of these musicals were written by his brother, Ira. In 1924, he became famous as a 'serious' composer when he wrote *Rhapsody in Blue*, for piano, jazz band and orchestra. One of his best-known works is the American folk opera, *Porgy and Bess*, which uses elements of jazz and blues.

Franz LISZT (1811-1886)

The Hungarian composer Liszt was one of the best pianists of his time and he composed some of the most difficult piano music ever written. He was already an established pianist by the age of 12. While he was studying composition in Paris, he began to write difficult music for piano. He was very impressed by the violinist, Paganini, and tried to make his piano music sound as spectacular as the music he played. Liszt toured many countries giving concerts, and huge audiences flocked to see him perform. Towards the end of his life, he moved to Rome where he spent the rest of his days teaching, composing and performing. He invented the term 'symphonic poem', for orchestral works that paint a picture or tell a story.

Jean-Baptiste LULLY (1632-1687)

Born in Italy, Lully went to Paris in 1646, and in 1653, he was employed at the court of King Louis XIV of France, where it was his job to provide music for the King's entertainment. His fame as a dancer, comedian and composer grew rapidly. He wrote operas, ballets and dance music, as well as religious music. He had to compose lots of ballet music as Louis himself was an enthusiastic dancer and often took part in court ballets. Most of Lully's music sounds very stately to reflect the pomp and grandeur of the court, and practically all his music was written to suit the tastes of the King.

Guillaume de MACHAUT (Around 1300-1377)

Machaut was a Medieval French composer and poet. He went to work for John of Luxembourg, King of Bohemia, around 1323. Soon after, he became a priest, but he continued to work for the King until the King died in 1346. He then served different French noblemen, including John, Duke of Berry. Machaut's music includes lots of religious music and songs, many of which are settings of his own poems.

Wolfgang Amadeus MOZART (1756-1791)

Born near Salzburg, in Austria, Mozart was a musical prodigy who was already composing at the age of five. During Mozart's childhood, his ambitious father took him and his sister Nannerl on several tours of Europe, where the gifted musicians gave concerts at many royal courts. The young Mozart astonished audiences with his musical skills. Later, in 1779, he worked in Salzburg, playing and composing for the Salzburg cathedral and court, but he quarrelled with his employer and left. He then moved to Vienna where he spent the rest of his life teaching, publishing his music, performing and composing. He earned a good salary, but still managed to get himself into debt. Mozart's music was much admired and Haydn once described him as 'the greatest composer known to me in person or by name'. He composed lots of different types of music: operas, oratorios, symphonies, concertos, chamber music, sonatas and settings of the mass. His operas were especially successful, and many are still popular today. Some of his most famous operas include *Le Nozze di Figaro* (The Marriage of Figaro), *Die Zauberflöte* (The Magic Flute) and *Don Giovanni*.

Modest Petrovich MUSORGSKY (1839-1881)

The Russian composer, Musorgsky, has often been described as the most original and influential member of 'The Russian Five'. He joined the army when he was only 13, but he had to resign a few years later because of problems with his nerves. He concentrated on composing instead. Some of his most famous works include his opera *Boris Gudunov*, and *Pictures at an Exhibition* for piano. He never finished many of his works, though, because of his heavy drinking, which resulted in his death when he was only 42.

Gioachino ROSSINI (1792-1868)

Rossini is one of the most popular composers of the 19th century. He is best known for his operas, and some of his most famous include *Tancredi*, *Guillaume Tell* and *Il barbiere di Siviglia*. He was taught to play the horn and to sing by his parents, who were both musicians in Bologna, in Italy, where the family lived. He sang in at least one opera when he was very young, and when he was 18, he began to write his own operas. Once he began receiving commissions to compose, Rossini wrote seven operas in 16 months. He continued to be very prolific and, in the years that followed, he composed almost 40 operas for opera houses in Naples, Milan, Paris and other European cities. When he was only 37, he became very ill and never wrote another opera.

Arnold SCHOENBERG (1874-1951)

Schoenberg was one of the most influential composers of the 20th century. For a long time, he was regarded as an amateur, but eventually came to be recognized as a great composer. Born in Vienna, in Austria, his first works were influenced by Brahms and **Wagner**, but he soon began to experiment with keys and tonality, first writing atonal music and later developing 12-note, or serial, music.

Franz SCHUBERT (1797-1828)

Even though he was only 31 when he died, Schubert produced a huge amount of music during his life. By the time he was 17 he had already composed his first symphony, some quartets, piano pieces and an opera. Born in Vienna, in Austria, Schubert learned to play many different instruments as a child including piano, violin and organ, and also studied singing and composition. He became a school teacher, but soon gave it up and concentrated on writing music instead. During his lifetime, he was probably best known as a composer of songs, or *Lieder*, and for the beautiful melodies he wrote. But he also composed lots of other types of music including symphonies, string quartets and piano music. Some of his most famous compositions include 'The Trout' quintet, the ninth symphony, known as the 'Great' symphony, and the *Lieder Erlkönig*, *Gretchen am Spinnrade* and *Der Wanderer*.

Igor STRAVINSKY (1882-1971)

Stravinsky's most famous work is his revolutionary ballet *The Rite of Spring* (1913). It is felt by many to be the work responsible for shaping 20th century music. Born near St. Petersburg, in Russia, Stravinsky studied with another Russian composer, Rimsky-Korsakov, who influenced his early works. In 1910, he moved to France with the Ballets Russes company and wrote a lot of ballet music for them, including *The Firebird* and *The Rite of Spring*. He was forced to take refuge in Switzerland during World War I. But most of his music from this time, around 1914-1918, is based on Russian folk tales and songs. In 1939, Stravinsky moved to the U.S., where he began to write music for movies. Even into his mid-80s, he continued to compose, conduct and make gramophone records of his music. As well as ballet music, Stravinsky also wrote operas, orchestral and chamber music, music for voices, and piano music.

Pyotr Il'yich TCHAIKOVSKY (1840-1893)

Tchaikovsky, one of the most popular Russian Romantic composers, is best known for his ballet music, especially *Swan Lake*, *The Nutcracker* and *The Sleeping Beauty*. At 19, he went to work for the Russian Ministry of Justice, but left after four years to study music. His first symphony was extremely successful and he soon became very famous. He often based his music on Russian folk tunes. Even though he was so successful, Tchaikovsky was very unhappy. He died in 1893, and some people think that he may have committed suicide.

Antonio VIVALDI (1678-1741)

Born in Venice, in Italy, Vivaldi is probably best known for his concertos. He wrote over 550 of them, including *The Four Seasons*, a set of four violin concertos. He was a priest, who began his career working at a girls' orphanage in Venice, where he wrote music for the girls to play and sing. Lots of Vivaldi's music was published, and as a result, he became very famous in Europe. Visiting musicians often commissioned works from him.

Richard WAGNER (1813-1883)

Wagner is probably the most famous German opera composer. Before Wagner, operas consisted of a series of separate musical numbers. Wagner was the first composer to blend musical numbers together within an opera, so the dividing line between them wasn't so clear. He also tried to give drama, music, scenery, and even dance, equal importance in his works. Operas such as *Tristan und Isolde* and *Tannhäuser* were very advanced for the time, and 19th century audiences often had difficulties understanding his music. Even today, some people still find it complex and challenging. Around 1850, Wagner began work on his most famous compositions, a set of four operas called *Der Ring des Nibelungen* (The Nibelung's Ring). The set took 25 years to complete, and it takes 18 hours to perform. Thanks to the financial support of Wagner's friend, King Ludwig II of Bavaria, Wagner even arranged for a special opera house to be built for its first performance in Bayreuth, in Germany, in 1876.

MUSIC ON THE INTERNET I

There are thousands of websites on the Net with music to listen to. On some sites, you can listen to music while you are connected to the Internet, by a process called "streaming". On other sites, you can download music and listen to it whenever you want, without going online. The next four pages tell you more about streaming and downloading. For links to all the sites mentioned on these pages, go to **www.usborne-quicklinks.com**

GETTING STARTED

To hear sounds on the Internet, your computer must have speakers and a device called a sound card, which enables it to produce sound. Most Macs and multimedia PCs have built-in sound cards and speakers.

If you don't have a computer, you may find that your school, college or local library is already online. Alternatively, you could go to an Internet café, or cybercafé. Before you go, check that headphones are provided. If not, you could ask about bringing your own.

STREAMING

Lots of websites that include sound use a process called "streaming". This means that the sound plays directly to your computer, and the information is not being stored on your computer. To listen to streamed sound, you may need to download a program called a "plug-in" from the Internet. One of the most widely-used plug-ins is called RealPlayer®.

This is the RealPlayer® home page.

If you try to listen to streamed files and you do not have the necessary program, a message saying so will come up on screen. There is usually a link on the website that you can click on to download the program you need.

LISTENING TO FAMOUS BANDS

Some record company websites, online music stores, and artists' official and unofficial sites include streamed files of songs by famous bands and artists for you to listen to. Playing these streamed files is a good way of listening to music that you would normally have to pay for. Some of these websites also contain video clips, so you can watch the latest pop videos.

The official websites of the Stereophonics and the Fun Lovin' Criminals both have streamed music videos for you to watch.

ONLINE RADIO

Many radio stations have websites where you can listen to broadcasts online. Internet radio is a very good way of listening to music from different parts of the world. In **Usborne Quicklinks** you'll find links to web directories where you can find lots of stations around the world.

The home pages of UK radio station Jazz fm (left) and radio-locator, a radio station web directory (above)

86

MUSIC MAGAZINES

Most major music magazines have websites with news, reviews, interviews and sound clips of bands and artists. There are also links to bands' official and unofficial sites.

The website of the UK music magazine NME

If you are in a band yourself, you'll find useful resources on the Internet, including information on instruments and equipment, as well as reviews and links to manufacturers' websites. There's also advice on starting out as a band, including how to go about getting gigs and recording your music.

The Harmony Central website is a good resource for bands.

Internet links

For links to artists' websites, online radio stations, music magazines, and a virtual music studio where you can make your own music, go to **www.usborne-quicklinks.com**

MAKE MUSIC ON THE WEB

As well as listening to music on the Net, you can also make up your own music. Some sites have online music mixers, where you can try out your skills as a DJ, by mixing different sounds or by adding effects to an existing dance track. There are also great resources for songwriters on the Net. You'll find online songwriting courses, songwriting tips, advice on performing and recording your songs, and articles by famous songwriters.

You can create your own mixes with online music mixers like this one.

WEBCASTS

You can also listen to live concerts, called Webcasts, or Cybercasts. These are usually filmed and recorded, then broadcast on record company sites, radio station sites, or pop stars' official websites. Webcasts are sometimes advertised in online music magazines.

The Pet Shop Boys in a Webcast shown on the NME website

MUSIC ON THE INTERNET II

As well as listening to streamed files, which only play while you are connected to the Internet, you can also download music and store it on your computer. Be aware, though, that it is usually illegal to store music by most well-known artists without paying for it.

MP3 FILES

Playing streamed files is useful when you want to listen to sound immediately, but the sound quality usually isn't as good as a CD. Storing CD-quality sound on a computer uses up a lot of space, but it is possible to make files smaller.

The most popular CD-quality files are MP3 files. These files contain the same digital information as music CDs, except that MP3 files are compressed so they are smaller. Compressing the files doesn't affect the sound quality of the music.

MP3 PLAYERS

To play MP3 files, you need a special piece of software. If your computer is fairly new, it may already have a program, called a media player, which plays MP3s. On PCs, it is usually the Microsoft® Windows Media™ Player, and on Macs, it's usually a program called QuickTime. The easiest way to find out if you have this software is to try to play an MP3 by double-clicking on it. If it doesn't play, you'll need to download one of these programs from the Net.

You can listen to streamed sound, as well as MP3 files, on the QuickTime Media Player.

There are also special programs, called MP3 players, that play MP3 files. You can download these players from the Internet. Lots of MP3 websites have lists of players for you to choose from.

SEARCHING FOR MP3s

There are thousands of websites that feature MP3s. When you find music you would like to download, however, it's important to be aware that most music is in copyright. In the case of famous performers, this means you *may* have to pay to download it. Even if you find free songs, they may well be on the site illegally. So check that the site states clearly that you have permission to download the tracks you choose.

Sometimes, however, the sites of some record labels, music stores or artists offer "copyright-free" tracks for you to download. There is also lots of good music, often by new and up-and-coming bands, that you can download for free. Even if it's not by a famous artist, it should still give you a good idea of what a particular style of music is like. You might even discover new bands or artists you prefer listening to!

Download free music from the ArtistDirect website, Amazon.com and MTV.com

DOWNLOADING

Once you have found the MP3 file you want to download, if you are a Microsoft® Windows® user, use your right mouse button to click on the link. If you are a Macintosh user, click and hold down the mouse button. If you use Microsoft® Internet Explorer, choose *Save target as* from the pop-up menu that appears. If you use Netscape® Navigator, choose *Save Link as* from the menu. Specify the directory where you want to store the file. (It's a good idea to create a new folder on your computer, specially for MP3 files, before you start.) Click on *OK*.

PLAYING DOWNLOADED FILES

You can play MP3s by double-clicking on them. You can also play them by opening your MP3 player or media player and loading the file you want to play. A file can usually be loaded by choosing the *Open* or *Add* option from the File menu, then browsing through your files to find the MP3. The on-screen controls on most players are the same as the controls on ordinary CD players, but it's best to read the instructions on your player's website.

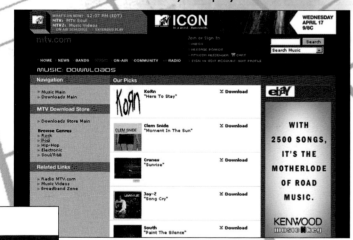

GETTING ORGANIZED

Lots of MP3 players and media players, such as the Windows Media™ Player (Version 7, or later versions), let you organize your files into lists, called playlists, so you can play them in the order you want. Some players even let you add videos and links to radio stations to your playlists.

You can create lots of different playlists on the Windows Media™ Player.

PORTABLE MP3 PLAYERS

As well as listening to MP3s on your computer, you can also transfer files onto tiny portable players and listen to them wherever you are, without using CDs or tapes. Portable MP3 players are like personal stereos, but most are even smaller. By connecting your portable player to your computer, you can copy the MP3 files you downloaded onto it, in whatever order you like.

Some mobile phones also work as portable MP3 players. By connecting an MP3 phone to your computer, you can copy downloaded files onto it, and then listen to the music through headphones.

This is a portable MP3 player.

Internet links

For links to websites where you can download music and find out about MP3 technology, go to **www.usborne-quicklinks.com**

GLOSSARY

If you can't find a word in this glossary, try looking it up in the index, as it may be explained elsewhere in the book. Words in **bold** type within the definitions have their own separate entries. Words in other languages, and words that originated in other languages, are printed in *italic* type.

acoustic instruments Instruments designed to produce and amplify sound without the help of electricity.

acoustics 1. The science of sound: the study of how sound behaves. 2. The acoustics of a concert hall, opera house, and so on, are the characteristics in its design, construction, fabric and decoration that affect the way sound is heard.

aleatory music Music which is open to interpretation on the part of the performer or composer. For example, the composer may decide which notes to use by throwing a dice, or the performer might select which sections of the piece to play.

alto Abbreviation for **contralto**, meaning the **vocal range** of the lowest female or boy's voice, or the highest adult male voice.

aria A type of song sung as part of an opera or **oratorio**

atonal Music that is not based around a key. Usually based around the **chromatic scale**, which uses all twelve notes.

Baroque The style of European music written between around 1600 and 1750.

bass The lowest male **vocal range**.

basso continuo An instrumental part common in the 17th and 18th centuries, consisting of a single line of music played on a low-sounding instrument such as a cello, double bass or bassoon. Another instrument, such as a harpsichord or organ, played chords based on this music. Symbols written above or below the music indicated a series of chords around which the player improvised.

bitonal A piece of music that uses two different keys simultaneously.

cadenza A showy passage within a **concerto** during which a soloist plays alone.

cantata A term used in the 17th century for a piece that was sung rather than played. Later, during the **Baroque** period, it came to mean a work for a choir with several solo singers, accompanied by an orchestra.

chamber music Music performed by a small group of musicians, each playing a separate part.

chromatic scale A **scale** of 12 notes, each a semitone apart.

chromaticism The inclusion of notes that are not part of the key in which a piece of music is written.

Classical music Serious or formal Western music. More specifically, it describes a style of Western music written between around 1750 and 1810.

concerto A piece for one or more solo instruments and an orchestra.

concerto grosso A **Baroque concerto** for a small group of instruments, called a *concertino*, with an orchestra, called a *ripieno*. Sometimes the *concertino* group played alone, and sometimes with the *ripieno* group.

contralto See **alto**

diatonic Any note or notes that belong to the scale of the key in which a piece of music is written.

dynamics The contrasts between loud and soft within a piece of music.

figured bass See *basso continuo*.

Impressionism A movement in art and music in the late 19th and early 20th centuries. Impressionistic music tries to convey moods and emotions rather than presenting a detailed musical picture.

improvisation Making up music as it is being performed.

instrumentation The choice of instruments used for a piece of music.

jam session An occasion when musicians, usually jazz musicians, work out the structure of a piece and **improvise** together.

libretto The words of an opera or **oratorio**.

Lieder The German for 'songs'. A term normally used for a type of 19th century song to be sung by a soloist with piano accompaniment.

madrigal A song for two to six voices which was popular during the Renaissance.

MIDI Abbreviaton for 'Musical Instrument Digital Interface'. A musician can record music into a computer system called a midi system. This enables the music to be stored as digital information. The information can then be used as instructions which tell a synthesizer how to play a piece of music.

minimal music A type of music, developed in the 20th century, that usually consists of lots of repetition of notes, phrases, rhythms or chords.

mode A type of **scale** used in Medieval and Renaissance times. Used today in many different types of traditional music.

musique concrète A style of music which developed in France in the late 1940s, involving the recording of natural sounds, then manipulating them in various ways to produce a piece of music.

mute A device fitted to an instrument, such as a violin, which muffles its tone by reducing its volume and **resonance**.

Nationalism A 19th and 20th century movement in which composers were influenced by the traditional music of their own countries. They wrote music based on, or including, elements of it.

Neo-classical music A style of 20th century music in which composers combined modern harmony and **tonality** with older Renaissance, **Baroque** or **Classical** forms.

note row The 12 notes in a **chromatic scale**, arranged and used as the basis for a piece of **serial music**.

opus The Latin for 'work'. Opus numbers given to musical works shows the order in which they were written or published.

oratorio A musical work for a choir, orchestra and solo singers, usually on a religious theme.

orchestration The arrangement of a piece of music for an orchestra.

pentatonic scale A five-note **scale**.

plainchant or **plainsong** Early church music, from the Medieval period, usually unaccompanied, consisting of sung Latin services.

polyphony Music consisting of a number of different tunes, which move independently, but weave together to form a harmonious whole.

ragas Sets of notes used as bases for **improvisation** in Indian music.

reed A strip of cane or metal used to make the sound in some woodwind instruments.

resonance The vibration of an object in response to sound wave vibrations close to it. Resonance amplifies the sound.

rhythm section Instruments, usually in a jazz band, which provide a steady beat, and **improvise** around this beat.

Romantic music Music written during the 19th century, which formed part of the Romantic movement in the arts. Composers tried to use music to express feelings and emotions, often inspired by nature, art and literature.

scale A set of notes on which a piece of music can be based. The name of a scale is determined by the pattern of intervals between the notes.

score A copy of a piece of music with all the instruments or voice parts arranged one above the other, so they can all be seen together.

serial music Music consisting of a **note row** repeated in various ways.

sonata A piece of music in three or four movements. Most *sonatas* are for a solo instrument or a small group of instruments.

song cycle A set of songs, or *Lieder*, linked by a theme, or telling a story.

soprano The highest female **vocal range**.

soundbox The body of an instrument designed to amplify the sound the instrument produces.

Sprechgesang German for 'speech song'. A style of singing which combines speech rhythms and tones with singing technique.

Sprechstimme German for 'speaking voice'. See *Sprechgesang*.

staff or **stave** A set of five lines on which musical notes are written. Each line, and space between the lines, represents a different pitch.

suite A set of separate pieces of classical music, often dances, designed to be played in sequence.

sympathetic strings Strings which resonate (see **resonance**) when other strings on the same instrument are plucked or bowed.

symphonic poem A large-scale work of descriptive music, not usually divided into separate movements.

symphony A large-scale work for orchestra, usually in three or four movements.

syncopation The placing of an emphasis in an unusual place in the bar, such as just before or after a main beat. This gives the music interesting tensions.

talas Sets of rhythm patterns used in Indian music.

tenor The highest male **vocal range**.

timbre The characteristic tone quality of an instrument.

tonality The tonality of a piece is its key. Tonality also refers to the major-minor key system as a whole.

tone poem See **symphonic poem**.

tone row See **note row**.

vibrato A rapid, small variation in the pitch of a note. It is used mainly by string players and singers to bring warmth and expression to the music.

virtuoso A brilliant instrumentalist or singer.

vocal range The difference in pitch between the lowest note a person can sing and the highest.

whole-tone scale A **scale** made up of six equal intervals of a tone each.

INSTRUCTIONS IN MUSIC

Many composers write instructions in their music to show you how they meant it to be played. As music was first printed in Italy, many musical terms are in Italian. Others are French or German. Some of the most common instructions are explained on this page. There is a guide with each entry to help you pronounce the instruction.

accelerando (ah-chel-eh-ran-doh) or *accel.* get gradually faster

adagio (ad-agi-oh) slow, at a leisurely pace

allegretto (ah-lay-gret-oh) not as fast as *allegro* and in a lighter style

allegro (ah-leg-row) quick, at a lively speed

andante (an-dan-tay) moderately slow, at a walking pace; a bit slower than *moderato*

andantino (an-dan-tee-no) faster and more lighthearted than *andante*. But, confusingly, it can also mean a little slower than *andante*

arco (ark-o) an instruction to string players to bow the strings (used after *pizzicato*)

a tempo (ah temp-o) an indication to return to the original speed after a change in speed, such as *rit., rall., accel.*

attacca (ah-tack-ah) attack; go straight on to the next section without a pause

cantabile (can-ta-bee-lay) in a singing style

con brio (con bree-o) vigorously, with spirit

con ped. (con ped) with pedal; instruction to pianists to use the sustaining (right-hand) pedal

crescendo (cresh-en-doh) or *cresc.* gradually getting louder (opposite of *decrescendo*)

da capo (da cap-oh) or *D.C.* from the beginning. Indication that the music is to be repeated from the beginning of the piece

da capo al fine (da cap-oh al fee-nay) repeat from the beginning, and end at the word *fine*

dal segno (dal sen-gno) repeat from the sign 𝄋

dal segno al fine (dal sen-gno al fee-nay) repeat from the sign 𝄋 and end at the word *fine*

decrescendo (dee-cresh-en-doh) or *decresc.* gradually getting quieter (see also *diminuendo*); opposite of *crescendo*

diminuendo (dim-in-u-en-doh) or *dim.* gradually getting quieter (see also *decrescendo*)

dolce (doll-chay) sweetly

fine (fee-nay) end

forte (for-tay) loud, strong

fortepiano (for-tay pee-ah-noh) loud, then immediately quiet

fortissimo (for-tih-see-mow) very loud

grave (grah-vay) very slow, serious

larghetto (lar-jet-oh) fairly slow and broad, but not as slow as *largo*

largo (lar-go) broad, at a stately speed

legato (leg-ah-tow) smooth (opposite of *staccato*)

lento (len-tow) slow

mezzo forte (metz-oh for-tay) moderately loud

mezzo piano (metz-oh pee-ah-no) moderately quiet

moderato (mod-er-ah-tow) at a moderate speed

pianissimo (pee-an-iss-ee-mow) very quiet

piano (pee-ah-no) quiet

pizzicato (pitz-ee-ka-tow) plucked; an indication to string players to pluck the strings with the fingertips rather than bow them

rallentando (ral-en-tan-doh) or *rall.* gradually getting slower (see also *ritardando*)

ritardando (rih-tar-dan-doh) or *rit.* gradually getting slower (see also *rallentando*)

staccato (stack-ah-tow) short, detached (opposite of *legato*)

tempo (tem-poh) speed

INDEX

ACKNOWLEDGEMENTS

MAINDEE 8/11/12

Every effort has been made to trace the copyright holders of the material in this book. If any rights have been omitted, the publishers offer to rectify this in any subsequent edition, following notification. The publishers are grateful to the following organizations and individuals for their contributions and permission to reproduce material (t=top, b=bottom, m=middle, l=left, r=right, bg=background):

Cover (violin) Howard Allman; (bg) © Digital Vision; (saxophone) © Stockbyte
p1 © Digital Vision
p2 Howard Allman
p3 (r) © Hulton-Deutsch Collection/CORBIS
p4-5 (bg) © Digital Vision
p4 (r) © Digital Vision
p6 (bg) © CORBIS; (b) © Keren Su/CORBIS
p7 (main) © Neal Preston/CORBIS; (tr) Courtesy of Columbia Records
p8-9 (bg) © Bettmann/CORBIS
p8 (main) © CORBIS; (tl) Courtesy of Sun Entertainment Corporation
p9 (tl) Craig Barritt/RETNA; (tr) Howard Allman; (b) © Apple Corps Ltd.
p10-11 (bg) © Bettmann/CORBIS
p10 (tl) Howard Allman; (b) © Gail Mooney/CORBIS
p11 (t) Action Press/Rex Features; (b) © Peter Turnley/CORBIS
p12 (tl) © Neal Preston/CORBIS; (b) © Denis O'Regan/CORBIS
p13 Mitchell Gerber/CORBIS
p14 © Digital Vision
p15 (tl) Tony Kyriacou/Rex Features; (bl) Ray Moller; (r) Gramophone: Paul Hoeffler/Redferns; (record sleeve) © Neil Preston/CORBIS; Record, cassette, CD, Mini Disc: Howard Allman; The Beastie Boys CD cover courtesy of Capitol Records Inc.; Rome MP3 Player courtesy of Rome Mp3
p16-17 (bg) © Bettmann/CORBIS
p16 (l) Howard Allman; (r) © Bettmann/CORBIS
p17 (r) © Roger Ressmeyer/CORBIS; (l) Howard Allman
p18-19 (bg) © Bettmann/CORBIS
p18 © Bettmann/CORBIS; (b) William Gottlieb/Redferns
p19 Philippe Halsman/Magnum Photos
p20 (t) © Otto Lang/CORBIS; (b, bg) © Archivo Iconografico, S.A./CORBIS
p21 (t) © Gianni Dagli Orti/CORBIS; (b) Explorer Archives/Mary Evans
p22-23 (bg) Ian Jackson
p22 (t) Mary Evans Picture Library; (b) Lebrecht Collection
p23 (l) © Bettmann/CORBIS; (r) © National Gallery Collection: By kind permission of the Trustees of the National Gallery, London/CORBIS
p24-25 (bg) © Digital Vision
p24 (t) © Bodleian Library, University of Oxford (2000), MS Douce 222, fols. 67v-68r; (b) © David Lees/CORBIS
p26-27 (bg) © Digital Vision
p26 (t) © Mitchell Gerber/CORBIS; (b) © Craig Lovell/CORBIS
p27 (t, bg) © Gianni Dagli Orti/CORBIS; (b) © Hulton-Deutsch Collection/CORBIS
p28 (t) © AKG/Schuetze/Rodemann; (b) © Michael Boys/CORBIS
p29 (tl) © Royal College of Music London; (tr, b) Lebrecht Collection
p30 (l) © Bettmann/CORBIS
p31 © Archivo Iconografico, S.A./CORBIS
p32-33 (bg) © Archivo Iconografico, S.A./CORBIS
p32 (l) © Archivo Iconografico, S.A./CORBIS; (r) Chris Stock/Lebrecht Collection
p33 (l) Toby Wales/Lebrecht Collection; (r) © CORBIS
p34-35 (bg) © Digital Vision
p34 (t) © Gianni Dagli Orti/CORBIS; (b) © Archivo Iconografico, S.A./CORBIS
p35 © Archivo Iconografico, S.A./CORBIS; (tr) © Archivo Iconografico, S.A./CORBIS; (br) © Archivo Iconografico, S.A./CORBIS
p36 © Gianni Dagli Orti/CORBIS
p37 (tr) Fritz Curzon/Performing Arts Library; (b) Concert for piano and orchestra by John Cage: © 1960 by Henmar Press Inc., New York. Reproduced on behalf of the publishers by permission of Peters Edition Ltd., London/Lebrecht Collection
p38-39 (bg) © Digital Vision
p38 (l) © Burstein Collection/CORBIS; (r) © Dean Conger/CORBIS
p39 (t) Des Willie/Redferns; (b) Odile Noel/Redferns
p40-41 (bg) © Shaen Adey, Gallo Images/CORBIS
p40 (t) © Peter Johnson/CORBIS; (b) © Peter Johnson/CORBIS

p41 (t) © Kennan Ward/CORBIS; (b) © CORBIS
p42-43 (bg) © Digital Vision
p42 (tl) © Bob Rowan, Progressive Image/CORBIS; (tr) © Tiziana and Gianni Baldizzone/CORBIS; (b) © Nik Wheeler/CORBIS
p43 (t) Howard Allman; (b) © Morton Beebe, S.F./CORBIS
p44-45 (main) Richard Megna/Fundamental/Science Photo Library
p44 Violin, trumpet: © Digital Vision; Saxophone: © Stockbyte
p45 (t) XBase09 drum machine reprinted with permission of JoMoX GmbH; (b) Trevor Boyer
p46 (tl) Lebrecht Collection; (ml) Lebrecht Collection (b); © Bettmann/CORBIS
p47 AKG London
p48-49 (bg) © Digital Vision
p48 © Digital Vision
p49 (l) Simone Burn/Performing Arts Library; (tr) Simone Burn/Performing Arts Library; (br) Clive Barda/Performing Arts Library
p50-51 (bg) © Archivo Iconografico, S.A./CORBIS
p50 (t) © Robbie Jack/CORBIS; (b) © Historical Picture Archive/CORBIS
p51 (l) Bill Cooper; (r) © E.O. Hoppé/CORBIS
p52 (bl) Audrey Zvoznikov/Hutchison Library; (bl, bg) © Digital Vision; (tr) Ann Johns
p53 (b) Retna
p54 (tl) Sasha Gusov/Performing Arts Library
p54-55 (b) Luigi Galante
p55 (r) © Robbie Jack/CORBIS
p56 (t) © Robbie Jack/CORBIS; (b) © Robbie Jack/CORBIS
p57 (tl) © Gianni Dagli Orti/CORBIS; (tr) Clive Barda/Performing Arts Library; (b) © Robbie Jack/CORBIS
p58-59 (bg) © Kurt Krieger/CORBIS
p58 (t) © Lynn Goldsmith/CORBIS; (b) © Mitchell Gerber/CORBIS
p59 (t) Ronald Grant Archive; (bl) © Shelley Gazin/CORBIS
p60 (bl) Ian Dickson/Redferns; (br) Dr. Jeremy Burgess/Science Photo Library
p61 (b) © Shelley Gazin/CORBIS
p62 (tl) Howard Allman; (tr) © Ted Spiegel/CORBIS; (b) Robert E. Daemmrich/Tony Stone
p63 (tl) © Digital Vision; (tr) Howard Allman; (ml) Howard Allman; (bl) © Adam Woolfitt/CORBIS; (br) © Bob Krist/CORBIS
p64 (t) Joe McEwan
p64-65 (b) Rotterdam Philharmonic Orchestra with chief conductor Valery Gergiev, Doelan Hall, Rotterdam: Wladimir Polak/Lebrecht Collection
p65 (t) © David Lees/CORBIS; (br) Clive Barda/Performing Arts Library
p66-71 Aziz Khan
p72 (l) Howard Allman; (tr) © Robert Holmes/CORBIS; (br) Howard Allman
p74-85 (bg) © Digital Vision
p80 (l) © Bettmann/CORBIS
p81 © Hulton-Deutsch Collection/CORBIS
p82 © Bettmann/CORBIS
p83-84 © Archivo Iconografico, S.A./CORBIS
p85 © Bettmann/CORBIS
p86-87 (bg) © Digital Vision
p86 (l) Courtesy of RealNetworks, Inc.; (tr) The Stereophonics screenshot courtesy of V2 Music Group; (tr) The Fun Lovin' Criminals screenshot courtesy of EMI Chrysalis; (br) Courtesy of Jazz FM; (br) With thanks to Radio-Locator
p87 (tl, br) Courtesy of NME.com; (bl) Used with permission of HarmonyCentral.com, Inc.; (tr) Courtesy of looplabs.com
p88-89 (bg) © Digital Vision
p88 (bl) Screenshots reprinted by permission from Apple Computer, Inc.; (tr) Courtesy of ARTISTdirect, Inc.; (br) © 2002 Amazon.com, Inc. All Rights Reserved
p89 (bl) © MTV Networks; (tr) Microsoft© Windows Media Player screenshot reprinted by permission from Microsoft Corporation; (br) Nomad II MP3 Player courtesy of CreativeLabs, Inc.
p90-93 © Digital Vision